Morning Has Broken

by
Jack Hywel-Davies

Fount
An Imprint of HarperCollins*Publishers*

First published in Great Britain
in 1991 by Fount Paperbacks

Fount Paperbacks is an imprint of
HarperCollinsReligious
Part of HarperCollins Publishers
77–85 Fulham Palace Road, London W6 8JB

Printed and bound in Great Britain by
HarperCollins Manufacturing, Glasgow

A catalogue record for this book
is available from the British Library

Morning Has Broken

To David Winter
with gratitude

Contents

Preface

'Morning Has Broken' can be heard every Sunday morning at half past six on BBC Radio 4. The considerable correspondence that floods into the production office every week is an indication of the popularity of a radio programme devoted to well-known hymns and sacred music.

There is no doubt that listeners appreciate the warmth that Jack Hywel-Davies brings to the programme with the soft Welsh lilt of his voice. Over the years he has discovered the background to most of the popular hymns that are sung today and this book represents the fruit of his labour.

I often hear it claimed that hymns are popular because they remind the older generation of their past. There is of course much truth in the claim — but not the whole truth. A great deal of popular music from the 1960s reminds me of my 'youth', but hymns that are many centuries old transcend even such personal nostalgia. They provide a tangible link with those Christians of past generations who used them to express the faith of Christ in their own day.

It is one of the astonishing facts of this secular age that there is a new vibrancy in Christian worship which has led to the publication of many contemporary hymns

and sacred songs. Not all of them will stand the test
of time, but then Charles Wesley wrote well over six
thousand hymns and I doubt if more than a tiny fraction
have survived to be sung regularly today.

Hymns and sacred songs are not fossilized relics of a
past age but part of a living Christian tradition. I hope
the information collected in this book will encourage
Christians to treasure that tradition and appreciate the
talents of writers and composers who struggle to
express something of the mystery of faith.

Stephen Oliver
Chief Producer, BBC Radio

Introduction —
The Stories of Hymns

As a Welshman I was raised on a rich menu of religious
music. This is not surprising as its history in Wales
stretches back a millennium and more. The Welsh mediaeval historian Giraldus Cambrensis, a distinguished
scholar and cleric of his day, made special reference to
part-singing in Wales long before it was accepted in
other parts of Europe. He once wrote:

> In their musical concerts the Welsh do not sing in
> unison like the inhabitants of other countries, but in
> many different parts; so that in a company of singers,
> which one very often meets with in Wales, you will
> hear as many different parts and voices as there are
> performers.

Hymns have one of the richest heritages of the printed
page from the times of the Israelites marching through
the wilderness and then using it as the Scots use their
bagpipes to scare the living daylights out of the Hittites,
Amorites and all the other 'ites' as they took possession
of the 'promised land'. They gave us all the *Songs of
Ascent* as in Psalm 121, and the solos with responses
from choirs as in Psalm 118, the magnificent 100th now
a prominent feature in all of today's hymn books, and

the glorious sound of praise from the 150th. Later when the temple was built the choirs were accompanied by large orchestras packed with talented musicians.

Jesus and his disciples sang hymns. They sang on the last Passover evening before Christ went to the Cross. There is a story in the apocryphal Acts of John which says that Jesus and the disciples sang their *gloria* holding hands standing in a ring. M. R. James in his *The Apocryphal New Testament* (page 253) says that the same book describes how Jesus begins to sing a hymn and then says, 'Glory to thee, Father', and the disciples answer, '*Amen*'. Then Jesus would sing again, 'Glory be to thee, Word: Glory be to thee, Grace', and the disciples would respond, '*Amen*'. Followed by Jesus singing, 'Glory be to thee, Spirit: Glory be to thee, Holy One: Glory be to thy Glory'. And the disciples, '*Amen*'. The book concludes with: 'Thus, my beloved, having danced with us, the Lord went forth.' On page 367 James describes what might be a novel way of handling insults. Referring to another apocryphal book called *The Acts of Thomas*, James says that when the apostle Thomas is insulted he responds by singing!

In modern times some of the most popular of all BBC religious programmes have been those featuring hymn-singing such as *Songs of Praise* and *Sunday Half-hour* and many listeners set their alarms to wake at 6.30 on Sunday mornings just to listen to the hymns in *Morning Has Broken*.

Perhaps the first *Morning Has Broken* programme occurred in the first century. In AD 112 the Roman Governor of Bithynia reported to Emperor Trajan that there was a Christian community that met at sunrise on the southern shores of the Black Sea to sing hymns!

Following the Reformation popular hymn-singing as we know it emerged through Watts and Wesley. Singing became so popular with the young Methodists that John Wesley gave them the following instructions:

Rules for Methodist Singers

1. Learn the tunes. **2**. Sing them as printed. **3**. Sing all. If it is a cross to you, take it up and you will find it a blessing. **4**. Sing lustily and with a good courage. **5**. Sing modestly. Do not bawl. **6**. Sing in time. Do not run before or stay behind. **7**. Above all, sing spiritually. Have an eye to God in every word you sing. Aim at pleasing him more than yourself or any other creature. In order to do this, attend strictly to the sense of what you sing and see that your heart is not carried away with the sound, but offered to God continually.

In contrast, Calvin pronounced hymns as idolatrous and that the church should only use words of Scripture hence the use of the metrical psalm. Although Calvin commissioned the French composer Louis Bourgeois to compose church music he then excommunicated him when he was too successful and began to harmonize the tunes.

Jefferson in his book *Hymns in Christian Worship* tells of the 'Slow Singers and the Quick Singers'. It appears that in the middle of the eighteenth century, when General Wolfe's troops were stationed in Aberdeen, it was their custom to hold their church parades in the cathedral. The troops sang the hymns with such gusto that the Aberdonians were so impressed that they invited one of the troopers, a Thomas Channon, to be their choirmaster. The succeeding success of the singing by the congregation attracted the attention of the University students who took to attending the services and singing with similar enthusiasm. But this annoyed a section of the congregation who believed that only psalms should be sung and then slowly and with what they called 'true dignity'. This section then resolved to silence the enthusiastic singers. Their plan was to seat three young urchins with shrill voices on the pulpit steps led by a youth named Gideon Duncan to sing out of tune during the service. Pandemonium ensued as the 'quick singers' battled with the 'slow singers'. The University students won the day, the boys were given a sound thrashing and the youth Duncan fined £50 by the local magistrate who imprisoned him until the fine was paid. Subsequently it became the practice to impose a fine of £50 to discourage bad singing.

I have been asked to explain the difference between an anthem and hymn-singing. The word is derived from the Greek 'anti' which means *against*, and the word 'phone' which is the word for *sound* or *voice*. This suggests a form of responsive singing called *antiphonal* for two or more voices. However, in the seventeenth century the word was sometimes used for solos, and then duets and quartets. Today the anthem can be a simple part-song or a short cantata sung by a choir as part of the worship service in a church.

Each week as I bury my head in my books reading the history of our hymns I am not only fascinated by the colourful characters I encounter in my journey of discoveries, but I am uplifted in my soul and enriched in mind by the lives of our hymn-writers both past and present.

Although in common with other ministers I have enjoyed selecting hymns for Sunday worship for many years, it was not until the Revd David Winter, then head of religious programmes for the BBC, introduced me to the Revd Stephen Oliver who is Chief Producer of the department, that I began a serious study of their background. This happened when Stephen invited me to present *Morning Has Broken*, and this book is one of the results. However, little did I realize at the time what a rich heritage they possessed.

The book is based on information I have dug out of many fields of resources, some not directly related to hymnology, which has made it difficult for me to respond to some of my listeners' requests for the sources of my information. Now, through the kind invitation of my friend Lesley Walmsley of HarperCollins, I hope that this book will go part of the way towards solving this problem.

Abide with me

1 Abide with me; fast falls the eventide;
   The darkness deepens; Lord, with me abide!
   When other helpers fail, and comforts flee,
   Help of the helpless, O abide with me.

2 Swift to its close ebbs out life's little day;
   Earth's joys grow dim, its glories pass away;
   Change and decay in all around I see;
   O thou who changest not, abide with me.

3 I need thy presence every passing hour;
   What but thy grace can foil the tempter's power?
   Who like thyself my guide and stay can be?
   Through cloud and sunshine, O abide with me.

4 I fear no foe with thee at hand to bless;
   Ills have no weight, and tears no bitterness.
   Where is death's sting? where, grave, thy victory?
   I triumph still, if thou abide with me.

5 Hold thou thy cross before my closing eyes;
   Shine through the gloom, and point me to the skies;
   Heaven's morning breaks, and earth's vain shadows
     flee;
   In life, in death, O Lord, abide with me!

Henry Francis Lyte who composed this hymn was born
in Ednam, near Kelso, Scotland on 1st June 1793. He
was educated at the Portora Royal School at Enniskillen,
Ulster and Trinity College, Dublin and distinguished
himself by winning the English poem prize on three
occasions. Though he first intended becoming a medical
doctor, after his graduation from Trinity in 1814 he was

ordained a deacon of the Church of England, and the following year he was appointed curate of Taghmon near Wexford. Subsequently he moved to Marazion, Cornwall, followed by a period in Lymington, Hampshire, and in 1823 he was installed as the perpetual curate of Lower Brixham, Devon, where he remained for the rest of his life. One little-known fact is that he shared a spiritual experience similar to that of the Wesley brothers. It happened one day that a priest in an adjoining parish was dying. He sent for Henry Lyte and confessed that he had lived a retrograde life and now feared meeting God. Together they searched through the Bible for some glimmer of hope, and the result was recorded by the hymnologist Julian in Lyte's own words:

The priest died happy under the belief that though he had deeply erred, there was One whose death and sufferings would atone for his delinquencies . . . I was greatly affected by the whole matter, and brought to look at life and its issue with a different eye than before; and I began to study my Bible, and preach in another manner than I had previously done.

Lyte lived in Berry Head House, the house given to him by King William IV, for the last twenty-four years of his life.

One version of how this hymn came to be written is that one Sunday evening in 1847 when Lyte preached his last sermon he went home and retired for a quiet time to his study.

His meditation that evening may well have centred around the very human story of Cleopas and his friend as told by Luke (chapter 24). Cleopas, like the other Jews, had read the old prophecies which foretold the coming of the Messiah to re-establish the kingdom of

Israel. For three years they had travelled with Jesus and listened to his teachings and had come to believe that he was the one to save Israel. But now he was dead and they began their journey home dejected and depressed. Luke then tells how Jesus joined them on their journey, but for some reason they didn't recognize him. During their journey he reminded Cleopas and his friend that the prophets also said that this Messiah would have to die first, and slowly the 'light' began to dawn on them. They began to feel good inside, and before they realized it, they were at the end of their journey but they felt strangely drawn to this stranger. So they begged him to stay the night in their home — 'Abide with us: for it is toward evening and the day is far spent.' Then, as they began to eat and he took the small loaf of bread and blessed it, they recognized him as Jesus. But before they could restrain him, he 'vanished out of their sight'. Some more modern versions translate these words as 'disappeared', but I prefer, 'he became *unseen* by them'. That says that he didn't really leave them, he was still there. It's just that they could not see him. An hour later Lyte came out of his study and handed some sheets of paper to a nearby relative which contained the victorious words, 'I fear no foe with Thee at hand to bless; ills have no weight, and tears no bitterness. Where is death's sting? Where, grave, thy victory? I triumph still, if Thou abide with me.'

All things bright and beautiful

*1 *All things bright and beautiful,*
 All creatures great and small,
 All things wise and wonderful —
 The Lord God made them all.

2 Each little flower that opens,
 Each little bird that sings —
 He made their glowing colours,
 He made their tiny wings.

3 The purple-headed mountain,
 The river running by,
 The sunset, and the morning
 That brightens up the sky,

4 The cold wind in the winter,
 The pleasant summer sun,
 The ripe fruits in the garden —
 He made them every one:

5 He gave us eyes to see them,
 And lips that we might tell
 How great is God Almighty,
 Who has made all things well.

Cecil Frances Alexander composed this hymn, like
many others she authored, for the benefit of children.
She was always concerned for children who were likely
to encounter difficulty in understanding the different
statements in the Creeds. With this in mind she devised
this method of making it easier and more attractive for
children to gain an understanding of the doctrine of the

* Verse 1 is also sung as a refrain after each other verse

Church of England. For example, when she wrote 'Once in royal David's city' her purpose was to explain the article in the Creed 'who was conceived by the Holy Ghost, born of the Virgin Mary'.

Another of her hymns which she composed with children in mind was, 'There is a green hill far away' which she based on the statement 'Suffered under Pontius Pilate, was crucified, dead and buried'. It's said she was inspired to write this hymn by a grass-covered hill which she used to pass near Londonderry in Northern Ireland. It was her custom in what today we would call 'market research' to read her hymns to her Sunday School children before passing them to her publisher, and on this occasion when she read the second line of the first verse, 'without a city wall', a little girl asked her what she meant by a green hill not having a city wall. But for some unknown reason she left the line unaltered. Now, however, it has been changed to 'outside a city wall' in many hymnals. She was born in Ireland in 1818 and was probably given her curiously masculine names from the strong military lines in both her parents' families. However, from an early age she was called Fanny, the second daughter of Major John Humphreys of the Royal Marines who served under Admiral Nelson.

In her teens she was attracted to the Oxford Movement and its richer style of worship than that of Irish Protestantism, and this brought her into contact with the Revd John Keble. This was reflected in many of her writings but due to the influence of the then Vicar of Leeds, the brilliant preacher Dr Hook, she refrained from adopting the extreme side of Anglo-Catholicism. I was interested to discover that Dr Hook was so successful as a preacher that he rebuilt his parish church in Leeds to accommodate a congregation of four thousand.

In 1843, when she was twenty-five years old, she wrote this hymn giving it the title 'Maker of Heaven and Earth' after the line in the Nicene Creed and based on the words in Genesis (1:31), 'And God saw every thing that he had made, and, behold, it was very good. And the evening and the morning were the sixth day.' Most hymnologists are now almost certain that she composed the hymn at Markree Castle at Colloney in Sligo, very close to the blue waters of the Atlantic at Ballysadare Bay. Two years later she married the curate William Alexander, later to become the Archbishop of Armagh.

One of the notable ways in which Mrs Alexander treated this subject with children in mind is that she avoided abstract statements, and confined herself to such real things that young minds could grasp, 'little flowers', 'birds that sing' and 'tiny wings'. The gentle application in the final verse is an invitation to worship God with such expressions as, 'He gave us eyes to see them and lips that we might tell how great is God Almighty'. Here God is seen as pleased with all that he had created, and that includes us as human beings. When we get depressed thinking we are of no value we would do well to remember that when God made this world, including us, he did not make rubbish! The other scriptural passages which are reflected in the hymn are Ecclesiastes 3:11 'He has made everything beautiful in its time', and John 1:3 'Through him all things were made; without him nothing was made that has been made' (NIV).

Amazing grace

1 Amazing grace — how sweet the sound —
 That saved a wretch like me!
 I once was lost, but now am found,
 Was blind, but now I see.

2 'Twas grace that taught my heart to fear,
 And grace my fears relieved;
 How precious did that grace appear
 The hour I first believed.

3 Through many dangers, toils and snares,
 I have already come;
 'Tis grace hath brought me safe thus far,
 And grace will lead me home.

4 When we've been there ten thousand years
 Bright shining as the sun,
 We've no less days to sing God's praise
 Than when we've first begun.

John Newton, the author of this hymn, along with William Cowper, gave us the Olney Hymns; Olney is the village in Buckinghamshire where Newton was appointed curate in 1764.

When he decided to enliven his services with hymns he grouped them into three sections. Book 1 comprised hymns based on collected verses of Scripture texts used to climax a sermon. Book 2 he called 'Occasional Subjects', which were poems relating to seasons or events in the Church calendar. In his introduction to Book 3 he says that these hymns were for 'the Progress and Changes of the Spiritual Life'.

The hymn 'Amazing grace' was placed in Book 1 and

the biblical reference which he used for it reveals how great a privilege he believed was given to him through the saving grace of Christ. It was 1 Chronicles 17:16 & 17: 'And David the king came and sat before the Lord, and said, "Who am I, O Lord God, and what is mine house, that thou has brought me hitherto? . . . for thou . . . regarded me according to the estate of a man of high degree." ' John Newton had lived a reprobate life which he personally described in his epitaph which he wrote in anticipation of his death. It can still be seen in the Church of St Mary Woolnoth, London, where he was Rector from 1780 until his death on 21st December 1807:

> JOHN NEWTON, CLERK, once an infidel and libertine, a servant of slaves in Africa, was by the rich mercy of our Lord and Saviour Jesus Christ preserved, restored, pardoned, and appointed to preach the Faith he had long laboured to destroy. Near sixteen years at Olney in Bucks, and twenty-seven years in this Church.

John's mother, a devout Christian, died when he was only seven years old and as his father was a seafaring captain he had no parental care for his formative years. At the age of eleven he put to sea with his father as an apprentice, and thereafter lived a wild and rebellious life. He was forced into service as a midshipman in a man-o'-war, but deserted, and thereafter roamed the seas ending up as captain of a ship trading in slaves. But one of the underlying influences for good in his reprobate life was the fact that when he was seventeen he fell in love with Mary Catlett when she was only fourteen years old and, in spite of the fact that her parents rightly did not consider him suitable for their daughter, he carried thoughts of her in his heart throughout his perilous travels. It was at this time that he was given a copy of *The Imitation of Christ* by the German monk, Thomas à Kempis, in which warnings of God's judgement are clearly written. Then he underwent a terrifying experience during a life-threatening storm when for hours on end he struggled to keep his vessel afloat. Both these events led to him calling upon God for mercy. It is no wonder that he later wrote: 'Through many dangers, toils and snares, I have already come; 'Tis grace hath brought me safe thus far, and grace will lead me home.' Forgiveness for John Newton not only changed his thinking enough for him to write these words of testimony to God's saving grace, but also for a tough, rough slave ship captain to compose the hymn, 'How sweet the name of Jesus sounds in a believer's ear! It soothes his sorrows, heals his wounds, and drives away his fear'.

He returned home to Liverpool a changed man, and on 10th February 1750 he married his childhood sweetheart, Mary, who had waited for him with hope in her heart. He took a land-based job as tide-surveyor, studied Hebrew and Greek and, even though some doubted his suitability, in 1758 applied for ordination in the Anglican Church. There was also a practical side to his Christian faith because in later life he joined forces with William Wilberforce in his campaign for the emancipation of the slaves. It is not without significance that the tune used for Newton's famous words, also called 'Amazing Grace,' began its life among the slaves in America's Deep South. The first known printing was in a publication called *Virginia Harmony* in 1831, but its popularity in this country, and subsequently worldwide, linked with John Newton's words, is due to its inclusion in a recording of the pipes and drums of the Royal Scots and Dragoon Guards. The other remarkable feature here was that the Guards chose the tune to fill the final gap on their long-playing record as a last-minute choice. I wonder what John Newton would have thought of the chances of his hymn-testimony heading the charts of the BBC's *Top of the Pops* for no less than nine weeks, and subsequently remaining in the charts for many additional months.

And didst those feet in ancient time

1 And did those feet in ancient time
  Walk upon England's mountains green?
  And was the holy Lamb of God
  On England's pleasant pastures seen?
  And did the countenance divine
  Shine forth upon our clouded hills?
  And was Jerusalem builded here
  Among those dark satanic mills?

2 Bring me my bow of burning gold!
  Bring me my arrows of desire!
  Bring me my spear! O clouds, unfold!
  Bring me my chariot of fire!
  I will not cease from mental fight,
  Nor shall my sword sleep in my hand,
  Till we have built Jerusalem
  In England's green and pleasant land.

The lines of this hymn come from William Blake's poem which first appeared written and and etched by himself in the Preface to his poem *Milton* early in the nineteenth century. It ends with a text from the Book of Numbers chapter 11: 'Would to God that all the Lord's people were prophets.' They were the words of Moses to Joshua when he complained that two of the Israelites were overstepping the mark and prophesying. In the Old Testament this meant one who speaks by the inspiration of God (Hebrew: nåbî), and this frequently happened at a time of national emergency. The Israelites, especially their kings, were mesmerized by their fascination for the prophets and repeatedly found themselves drawn to them. But they were rarely prepared for what the prophets would say to them. They wanted the prophets to confirm them in their self-opinionated ways. However, the true prophets, as opposed to the false prophets, would only say what they were inspired by God to proclaim to the king and his people. So when the prophets made the people uncomfortable, or even frightened, they foolishly stoned the prophets thinking that was the way to deal with their problems and prevent the fulfilment of the prophecy and the judgement of God falling upon them. Of course, the very reverse happened.

William Blake who was born in London in 1757, son of James Blake a hosier living at 28 Broad Street, Golden Square, London, was something of a prophet himself, as well as a fine artist and poet. He used to see visions and dream dreams. As his life developed so did his sense of the mission to present Christ as Saviour and the one to solve the world's problems.

I think it is worthy of note that his wife Catherine, whom he married in August 1782, was described as the perfect wife. She learned to draw and paint to a sufficiently high standard that she was able to help him in his work, which is probably why his output was so large; he completed his series of 537 water-colour designs for Young's *Night Thoughts* before he was forty. He died childless in 1827 and Catherine four years later.

In this hymn (though some hymnologists hesitate to classify it as a hymn) he draws on the imagery of the Bible plus his fertile imagination, and some say probably mixes with it one of the legends that Jesus accompanied Joseph of Arimathea on a visit to the British Isles and Cornwall in particular. This is based on his references to the 'holy Lamb of God on England's pleasant pastures' and new Jerusalem 'builded here'. But he set it in the form of questions. One historian said of him that in his books 'his lyrical and mystical elements were intimately mingled' and his 'mystical and metaphysical systems' proved a stumbling-block to most of his readers. So I prefer to believe that Blake, in spite of his fanciful references to the legend, had in mind a picture of the new Jerusalem in John's Book of Revelation as it descended from heaven. And then emerges the prophetical side of Blake as he turns his verse into a rallying call for the prophets of his day to herald its coming. So I can only guess that his poem was meant as a call to all (hence his reference to the words of Moses to Joshua), irrespective of rank, to serve his country in the name of Christ his Saviour.

The line, 'I will not cease from mental fight', appealed to the Christian Socialists of the 1880s who printed it in the monthly paper of their society, *The Guild of St Matthew*.

The poem only came to public notice after Sir Hubert Parry composed the tune for Blake's words at the request of Dr Robert Bridges. When Sir Hubert completed his composition he handed the manuscript to his friend, Sir Walford Davies, with this delightful throwaway line: 'Here's a tune for you, old chap. Do what you like with it.' I was pleased to have this intimate story confirmed by Sir Walford's nephew, John Wilson, when I visited him in his Guildford home recently.

Blake's words set to Parry's tune were first used in 1916 for a meeting in Queens Hall, Langham Place, London, where Sir Henry Wood first held his promenade concerts after his appointment as conductor of the newly formed Queen's Hall Orchestra (1895). The hall was destroyed in an air raid during the Second World War (1941) and now on that site stands St George's Hotel and a building which houses the BBC library which has been an excellent resource centre for this book and my broadcasts.

Two years later (March 1918) Blake's 'Jerusalem' was used again for a service of thanksgiving in the Royal Albert Hall to celebrate Parliament's 7-to–1 vote in

favour of Women's Suffrage. And maybe that is why
for some years it was sung so enthusiastically at the
annual gatherings of the ladies of the Women's
Institute.

As with gladness men of old

1 As with gladness men of old
  Did the guiding star behold,
  As with joy they hailed its light
  Leading onward, beaming bright –
  So, most gracious Lord, may we
  Evermore be led to thee.

2 As with joyful steps they sped,
  Saviour, to thy lowly bed,
  There to bend the knee before
  Thee, whom heaven and earth adore –
  So may we with willing feet
  Ever seek thy mercy-seat.

3 As they offered gifts most rare
  At thy cradle rude and bare –
  So may we with holy joy,
  Pure, and free from sin's alloy,
  All our costliest treasures bring,
  Christ, to thee, our heavenly King.

4 Holy Jesus, every day
  Keep us in the narrow way;
  And, when earthly things are past,
  Bring our ransomed souls at last
  Where they need no star to guide,
  Where no clouds thy glory hide.

5 In the heavenly country bright
  Need they no created light;
  Thou its light, its joy, its crown,
  Thou its sun which goes not down;
  There for ever may we sing
  Alleluias to our King.

It was probably the evening of Epiphany day in 1860 that the son of Dr W. J. Dix of Bristol greeted his father's return home from attending service in St Raphael's Church with this observation on St Matthew's account of the birth of Jesus: 'This business of three kings from the Orient just is not true. It's merely part of the tradition that grew up around the birth of our Lord and has no biblical basis whatsoever. So I've written some verses for a new hymn on the subject.' 'I'm curious', said Dr Dix to his son William Chatterton, who had been obliged to remain at home convalescing from a sickness. 'May I hear what you've written?' So William read, 'As with gladness men of old did the guiding star behold, as with joy they hailed its light, leading onward, beaming bright – so, most gracious Lord, may we evermore be led to thee.' 'I see you referred to the easterners as "men" instead of "wise men" or "kings" ', observed his father. 'I did it on purpose', said the young man, 'so that no one could challenge the authenticity of my statement.'

William Chatterton Dix, so named by his doctor father after his favourite poet William Chatterton, was a devout Christian in the high church tradition of the Anglican Church. He was an able linguist and versifier of the old hymns of Greece and Abyssinia, especially those translated by Dr Littledale. He was also a hymn-writer in his own right, and gave us the worshipful eucharist hymn, 'Alleluia, sing to Jesus', which he wrote for ascensiontide. It is interesting to note that though a high churchman he placed special emphasis on the Bible above that of tradition, also emphasizing the humanity as well as the divinity of Jesus in his altar songs. His business life took him to Glasgow as the manager of a marine insurance company.

There are several theories as to the origin of the men from the east who brought gifts to the infant Christ at Bethlehem located on a high ridge over 2000 feet above

sea level some five miles south of Jerusalem. There were
four political districts in Israel and this Bethlehem was
the one in Judea. This is significant because of the
prophecy in Micah 5:2. Their description as 'wise' and
'kings' and 'three' does not, as Dix told his father, have
any foundation in the Scriptures. Whilst it can safely
be assumed that the *magi* who came from the east were
wise because of their knowledge of the heavens, it is
highly doubtful that there would have been only three,
or that they were kings. Travellers through the deserts
of the Orient would never take long journeys in small
groups because of the danger of attack from robbers.
Furthermore it is likely that a large retinue arriving in
Jerusalem would attract the attention of someone like
King Herod. It is more likely that the number *three*
grew up in tradition on account of the three gifts: gold,
frankincense and myrrh.

The worship of Jesus is the strong emphasis of this
hymn. Sometimes we dwell on what we are able to do
for God as the most significant, but here in this hymn,
supported by many incidents in the Bible, worship and
praise always transcend our activities. Two classic
examples are the stories of Mary and Martha in Luke
10:38–42 and Mary's adoration of our Lord through the
anointing with ointment of Jesus' feet described by St
John in his Gospel 12:3–7. Comparing the gifts of the
men from the east with what we should do, the hymn-
writer says, 'So may we with holy joy, pure, and free
from sin's alloy, all our costliest treasures bring, Christ,
to thee, our heavenly King.'

Be thou my vision

1 Be thou my vision, O Lord of my heart;
  Naught be all else to me, save that thou art –
  Thou my best thought, by day or by night,
  Waking or sleeping, thy presence my light.

2 Be thou my wisdom, thou my true Word;
  I ever with thee, thou with me, Lord;
  Thou my great Father, I thy true son;
  Thou in me dwelling, and I with thee one.

3 Be thou my battle-shield, sword for the fight,
  Be thou my dignity, thou my delight.
  Thou my soul's shelter, thou my high tower:
  Raise thou me heavenward, O Power of my power.

4 Riches I heed not, nor man's empty praise,
  Thou mine inheritance, now and always,
  Thou and thou only, first in my heart,
  High King of heaven, my treasure thou art.

5 High King of heaven, after victory won,
  May I reach heaven's joys, O bright heaven's Sun!
  Heart of my own heart, whatever befall,
  Still be my vision, O ruler of all.

For this highly spiritual hymn we are indebted to two women, one from Dublin, Eire and the other from Manchester, England, both highly qualified specialists in ancient Irish writings from where they derived these lines. The Irish lady was Mary Elizabeth Byrne, or as she was known in Gaelic, *Maire ni Bhroin*, who was born in Dublin on 2nd July 1880. She was educated at the Dominican Convent in Eccles Street and the Univer-

sity of Ireland where she obtained her MA in 1905 and
the Chancellor's Gold Medal. She specialized in the
Irish language and edited ancient Irish writings, becoming one of the editors of the *Old and Mid-Irish Dictionary*
of the Royal Irish Academy. One of her translations
into English was an eighth-century Irish poem, *Rob tu
mo bhoile, a Comdi cride*, two copies of which are retained
in the Royal Irish Academy library. Her literal translation was published in 1905 in the journal of the School
of Irish Learning, *ERIU*, with the appropriate title, 'A
Prayer'. She died in her native Dublin on 19th January
1931.

The English lady was Eleanor Henrietta Hull, who
was born in Cheetham in Manchester on 15th January
1860, into an academic family; her father was a university professor. She was educated at Alexandra College
and the Royal College of Science, Dublin, where she
studied under Holgar Pederson and Kuno Meyer. Her
whole life was taken up with the study of Irish art and
culture, and I find her name as a contributor in my
volumes of Hastings' *Encyclopaedia of Religion and Ethics*.
She served many Irish literary societies, the Royal Asia-
tic Society and the Folklore Society. She also edited a
series of books, *Lives of the Celtic Saints*. Miss Hull came
across Miss Byrne's translation not very long after it
was published and decided to produce a metrical version. She skilfully converted Mary's prose into verse,
preserving much of her phrasing.

It is a very personal prayer for a clear sight of God,
with wisdom, truth and protection for the way ahead
coupled with an act of dedication to the service of God.
It also expresses the ageless need of man to have a
heavenly vision, to experience God's care and personal
presence throughout his earthly pilgrimage. And in that
connection I think it is worth quoting another lady,
Katherine Logan, who once wrote: 'Vision is of God. A
vision comes in advance of any task well done.'

The hymn was published in London in 1912, set out in couplets, in Eleanor Hull's *Poem-Book of the Gael*. She was living in Wimbledon, Surrey, when she died on 13th January 1935.

The tune to which this poem is invariably sung is known as 'Slane'. There is an interesting legend told about this part of Ireland which I think is worth repeating. It may not be based on proven fact, so you can look upon it as a parable that supports the thoughts expressed in the hymn.

Slane is the name of a hill about ten miles from Tara, County Meath, where the story goes that St Patrick and his white-robed companions confronted the pagan King Leogaire MacNeill. The king followed the religion of the Druid fire-worshippers and decreed that he was to be the first to light the fire on Tara in the springtime of the year. But Patrick beat him to it, by lighting the Pascal-fire on Slane in honour of Christ. When the king saw it he was angry and sent for Patrick, planning an ambush for him and his followers en route. However, as the saint and his followers approached the king's seat at Tara they were made to look like deer and arrived safely. Then, turning the tables on the king, St Patrick converted him to Christianity!

Christ is the world's light, he and none other

1 Christ is the world's light, he and none other;
  Born in our darkness, he became our brother.
  If we have seen him, we have seen the Father:
  Glory to God on high.

2 Christ is the world's peace, he and no other;
  No man can serve him and despise his brother.
  Who else unites us, one in God the Father?
  Glory to God on high.

3 Christ is the world's life, he and no other;
  Sold once for silver, murdered here, our brother,
  He, who redeems us, reigns with God the Father:
  Glory to God on high.

4 Give God the glory, God and no other;
  Give God the glory, Spirit, Son and Father;
  Give God the glory, God in man my brother:
  Glory to God on high.

This was written by one of our contemporary hymn-writers, a Methodist minister born in 1903 in the village of Roby, now part of Liverpool, whose father ran a successful leather-manufacturing business. He is the Revd Fred Pratt Green, both poet and hymn-writer. He is the child of a Wesleyan Methodist home, educated at the Methodist Public School, Rydal, Colwyn Bay, and a member of Claremont Road Wesleyan Church, Wallasey. As I was also born into a Wesleyan Methodist family I have always thought them to be the true-blood Methodists! Fred entered the Methodist ministry in 1928 and in his first assignment as chaplain to the Methodist

boarding school for girls at Hunmanby Hall in Yorkshire
achieved the distinction of a 'double-first' — he composed his first hymn, 'God lit a flame in Bethlehem',
and fell in love with the school's French mistress,
eventually marrying her!

In 1944, after a number of pastorates, he arrived in
the Methodist Circuit of Finsbury Park where he met a
cripple who was to be a further inspiration to his poetic
gifts. Fallon Webb was the father of one of Fred's
Sunday School scholars. Though crippled with arthritis
Fallon was consumed with an interest in poetry, and
suggested to his son's pastor that they exchange their
writings from time to time for critical examination. This
they did for twenty years until Fallon died, by which
time Fred was a better poet, and we in the churches
had also gained from his supply of hymns. However, I
hasten to add that Fred makes a distinction between
the two in his latest book (*Later Hymns and Ballads and
Fifty Poems*, 1989: publishers Stainer and Bell) in which
he writes:

> The poet, as such writes to please himself. His vision
> is personal and private. And he is rarely a con-
> formist . . . The hymn-writer, in contrast, does not
> write to please himself. He is a servant of the Church.

Fred Pratt Green entitled this hymn 'The uniqueness of
Christ' — Christ is the world's Light, he and none other;
born in our darkness, he became our brother. If we
have seen him, we have seen the Father.

It is set to a French church melody from the *Paris
Antiphoner* of 1681, harmonized by Ralph Vaughan
Williams.

It was introduced to the congregation of the Vale
Royal Methodist Church, Tunbridge Wells at their harvest thanksgiving service in September 1968, and
chosen as the only contemporary hymn for the inaugur-

ation service at Westminster Abbey for the Congregational and Presbyterian Churches. It has since been translated into several other languages with the distinguished theologian Karl Barth being involved in the German translation.

The hymn features strong biblical images of Christ as the world's Light, Peace and Life. The many scriptures reflected in the hymn are the first chapters of two of St John's epistles, his Gospel and the Book of Revelation. Then in verse four of the hymn there is a joyous acclamation of the Trinity. It is altogether a magnificent hymn which is why it is widely used by people of all religious denominations.

Christians, awake

1 Christians, awake, salute the happy morn,
  Whereon the Saviour of the world was born;
  Rise to adore the mystery of love,
  Which hosts of angels chanted from above;
  With them the joyful tidings first begun
  Of God Incarnate and the Virgin's Son:

2 Then to the watchful shepherds it was told,
  Who heard the angelic herald's voice, 'Behold,
  I bring good tidings of a Saviour's birth
  To you and all the nations upon earth;
  This day hath God fulfilled his promised word,
  This day is born a Saviour, Christ the Lord.'

3 To Bethl'em straight the enlightened shepherds ran
  To see the wonder God had wrought for man,
  And found, with Joseph and the blessed Maid,
  Her Son, the Saviour, in a manger laid;
  Joyful, the wondrous story they proclaim,
  The first apostles of his infant fame.

4 O may we keep and ponder in our mind
  God's wondrous love in saving lost mankind;
  Trace we the Babe, who hath retrieved our loss,
  From his poor manger to his bitter cross;
  Saved by his love, incessant we shall sing
  Eternal praise to heaven's almighty King.

One day late in the year 1749 a loving and indulgent
father said to his little daughter, Dolly, 'What would
you like me to give you for Christmas?' 'Please write
me a poem', was the surprising reply. And so it was
that on Christmas Day 1749 when young Dolly came

down to breakfast in her Manchester home she found a sheet of paper on her plate on which was written, 'Christmas day for Dolly', and underneath a poem of forty-eight lines beginning, 'Christians, awake, salute the happy morn, whereon the Saviour of the world was born.'

The next part of the story is just as fascinating. John Wainwright, the organist of the parish church of nearby Stockport, who was an acquaintance of Dolly's father, John Byrom, was given sight of the poem in the following months and, it appears, without their knowledge composed the tune 'Yorkshire' for it.

So it was that on the morning of the following Christmas Day the Byrom family were awakened by hearing Dolly's 'Christmas present' being sung under their bedroom windows by Mr Wainwright and his choir, and John Byrom entered in his diary for Christmas 1750: 'The singing men and boys, with Mr Wainwright, came here and sang "Christians, awake".'

No one knows why the tune was given the name 'Yorkshire' when its composer was from Lancashire, especially as he first gave it the name 'Stockport', the place where he was born. In fact, a nonconformist parson called Caleb Ashworth, from Daventry, hijacked the tune and published it as a psalm tune without the composer's permission, and when challenged excused himself by saying that he was only giving the tune free advertisement! This prompted John Wainwright to publish it himself with John Byrom's words.

John Byrom, who was born in 1692, was one of the eighteenth century's most colourful personalities. He reckoned that he had only ever met two other people in Britain who were taller than himself. No one could mistake him with his long Dutch nose and protruding neck as he walked through Manchester carrying a long cane and wearing a broad-brimmed slouch hat. He was a surgeon, having qualified at the University of

Montpellier in France where he lived as a refugee to which place he had to escape for fear of arrest because of his allegiance to the 'Pretender' of the House of Stuart.

He was an Anglican who favoured the Arminian teachings of the Wesleys. He also invented a system of shorthand which he taught the Wesleys. Charles became so proficient that he used it for his famous journals, and composed most of his hymns in that way. It was also officially taught at both Oxford and Cambridge Universities and even used by the Clerk of the House of Lords endorsing the system with the following inscription: 'On 16th June 1742 His Majesty George II secured to John Byrom, MA, the sole right of publishing for a certain term of years (twenty-one) the art and method of shorthand invented by him.'

Byrom's intellectual stature was recognized by his election as a Fellow of the Royal Society when Isaac Newton was its President. He was also not without a sense of humour. In one of his many volumes he stated his theological position with the following bit of doggerel:

> Flatter me not with your *Predestination*,
> Nor sink my spirits with your *Reprobation*.
> From all your high disputes I stand aloof,
> Your *Pre's* and *Re's*, your *Destin* and your *Proof*,
> And formal, *Calvinistical* Pretense,
> That contradicts all Gospel and good Sense.

When his brother died he inherited the family property in Manchester in 1724 and became one of its most influential inhabitants and renowned for his Jacobite sympathies expressed in his famous epigram:

God bless the King — I mean the Faith's Defender;
God bless (no harm in blessing) the Pretender,

But who Pretender is, or who is King,
God bless us all! that's quite another thing.

He died in his beloved Manchester on 26th September
1763.

Count your blessings, name them one by one

1 When upon life's billows you are tempest tossed,
  When you are discouraged, thinking, all is lost,
  Count your many blessings, name them one by one,
  And it will surprise you what the Lord hath done.
  Count your blessings, name them one by one,
  Count your blessings, see what God hath done;
  Count your blessings, name them one by one,
  And it will surprise you what the Lord hath done.

2 Are you ever burdened with a load of care?
  Does the cross seem heavy you are called to bear?
  Count your many blessings, every doubt will fly,
  And you will be singing as the days go by.

3 When you look at others with their lands and gold,
  Think that Christ has promised you his wealth
    untold,
  Count your many blessings, money cannot buy
  Your reward in heaven, nor your home on high.

4 So amid the conflict, whether great or small,
  Do not be discouraged, God is over all,
  Count your many blessings, angels will attend,
  Help and comfort give you to your journey's end.

Classical hymnists may dismiss this as a sugary pop-
song of the mission hall category, so I was pleasantly
surprised to read that it was one of the most frequently
sung hymns during the 1904 Welsh Revival along with
'Guide me, O thou Great Jehovah'. Gypsy Smith was
reported by the newspaper of the day, *The London Daily*,
as saying of the hymn, 'In South London the men sing

it, the boys whistle it, and women rock their babies to sleep on this hymn.'

It was written by the Revd Johnson Oatman, Junior, probably the most prolific writer of sacred songs around the turn of this century. He authored between three and five thousand hymns or sacred songs in his lifetime of sixty-eight years but apart from this hymn and another which begins, 'I'm pressing on the upward way, new heights I'm gaining every day', none of them appears in our hymn-books. Interestingly, this hymn is listed by The Hymn Society as being in the *Redemption Hymnal, Salvation Army Hymn Book*, and surprisingly, *The Mirfield Mission Hymn Book* of 1936. Mirfield is in the Anglo-Catholic arm of the Church of England.

Oatman was born in New Jersey in April 1856 and became a member of the Methodist Episcopal Church at nineteen years of age. He was later ordained and licensed to preach, but he never pastored a church. He was thirty-six when he started writing hymns, which averaged between four and five a week, and apparently he was paid a dollar for each of them.

'Count Your Blessings' was written with young people in mind and the experiences they would be likely to face during their life's journey. The first verse draws its imagery from the experience of the disciples in their storm-tossed ship as described by Mark 4: 37–40:

And there arose a great storm of wind, and the waves beat into the ship, so that it was now full. And he was in the hinder part of the ship, asleep on a pillow: and they awake him, and say unto him, Master, carest thou not that we perish? And he arose, and rebuked the wind, and said unto the sea, Peace, be still. And the wind ceased, and there was a great calm. And he said unto them, Why are ye so fearful? how is that ye have no faith?

And so Oatman wrote, 'When upon life's billows you are tempest tossed, When you are discouraged, thinking all is lost, count your many blessings . . .' The main blessing that these disciples possessed, but did not realize at the time, was the privilege and protection of having Jesus in the boat — with them in the storm!

Peace is a blessing which is available to the Christian free of charge, which means that it does not depend on his bank balance, or a high-powered job in the city, or a fine house in the country. For me this peace has three compartments: (1) The peace of God, which comes through having; (2) the peace of God, which results in men and women having; (3) peace not only within but also round about, i.e. in the family, the community and ultimately in the world. As Paul wrote to the Christians in Ephesus, 'Blessed be the God and Father of our Lord Jesus Christ, who hath blessed us with all spiritual blessings in heavenly places in Christ' (Ephesians 1: 3). 'Count you many blessings' was first published in 1897 by Edwin Excell in a book entitled *Songs for Young People*. In fact, Mr Excell composed the music for the words. He was well known for his work in gospel music as composer, teacher, publisher and in his early days song leader for different evangelists. He was born in Stark County, Ohio, in December 1851 and wrote the music for over 2000 gospel songs and published fifty songbooks. He was with Gypsy Smith in his evangelistic campaign in Louisville, Kentucky, still leading the music at the age of seventy when he suddenly passed to be with his Lord.

Dear Lord and Father of mankind, forgive our foolish ways

1 Dear Lord and Father of mankind,
  Forgive our foolish ways;
  Re-clothe us in our rightful mind;
  In purer lives thy service find,
  In deeper reverence, praise.

2 In simple trust like theirs who heard,
  Beside the Syrian sea,
  The gracious calling of the Lord,
  Let us, like them, without a word
  Rise up and follow thee.

3 O Sabbath rest by Galilee!
  O calm of hills above,
  Where Jesus knelt to share with thee
  The silence of eternity,
  Interpreted by love!

4 Drop thy still dews of quietness,
  Till all our strivings cease;
  Take from our souls the strain and stress,
  And let our ordered lives confess
  The beauty of thy peace.

5 Breathe through the heats of our desire
  Thy coolness and thy balm;
  Let sense be dumb, let flesh retire;
  Speak through the earthquake, wind, and fire,
  O still small voice of calm!

This hymn comes from a poem by John Greenleaf Whittier who was born on 17th December 1807 in the Merimac Valley of East Haverhill, in Massachusetts, in a big farmhouse that today is a pilgrim shrine. His parents were farmers and Quakers. When he was a young lad a singing pedlar visiting his village caught his attention, from whom he bought a book of poems by Robert Burns which sparked in him a desire to write verse.

By the time he was fourteen Whittier was also writing poems, some of which were published in the Newburyport *Free Press* in 1824. William Lloyd Garrison, the editor, recognized John's talent and persuaded his father to send him to the Academy at Haverhill to study journalism. This led him to becoming a newspaper editor, but through illness he had to return to his father's farm where he worked in poor circumstances but still wrote at night for a period of five years. The farm was then sold and he moved to Philadelphia where, in 1838, he became editor of *The Pennsylvania Freeman*.

As a result of his Quaker upbringing and the influence of his first editor, Garrison, he began using his writing skill in the cause of social justice with special emphasis on the abolition of slavery. He was attacked for this and his office burned.

He wrote many poems which, true to his Quaker upbringing, were not designed at first to be used as hymns although fifty of them subsequently found their way in our hymn-books. He died on 7th September 1892 at Hampton Falls in New Hampshire.

Part of the beauty of this hymn lies in the suggested pictures from the Bible in such phrases as 'reclothe us in our rightful mind'. This comes from Mark chapter 5, which recounts the story of the man possessed by demons who drove him out of his mind. After he was set free, forgiven and healed by Jesus, Mark says the man's 'fellow villagers found him clothed and in his right mind'. Another phrase, 'O still small voice of calm', refers to the time God spoke to Elijah on Mount Horeb (1 Kings 19:12). God caused a strong wind and an earthquake but did not speak in that way, instead he spoke 'in a still small voice'.

The verses of this hymn were taken from Whittier's poem of seventeen verses called *The Brewing of Soma* which was published in 1872.

The story behind the title is fascinating. Soma was a plant from which the Hindu priests used to make an intoxicating drink with honey and milk. After consecrating it with their rods it was pronounced as 'the drink of the gods'. It induced in the Indians a state of ecstasy, a storm of drunken joy as they noisily cavorted around worshipping their gods. It was also referred to as milk-wood, and I wonder if that is why Dylan Thomas, an inveterate drinker of alcohol, entitled his play *Under Milk Wood*?

But back to Whittier's poem. He wrote:

> From tent to tent
> The Soma's sacred madness went
> A storm of drunken joy

Whittier graphically describes the rites in which Soma is used and compares them with the 'still dews of quietness' which is how he worshippped God. However, he also recognizes that some Christians, without the intoxicating brew of Soma, could also behave in the same way as the Indians:

> In sensual transports
> Wild as vain
> We brew in many a Christian fane
> The heathen soma still

Whittier's lines encourage us to a restful worship of

God, a gentle meditation 'till all our strivings cease; take from our souls the strain and stress, and let our ordered lives confess the beauty of thy peace'.

Eternal Father strong to save

1 Eternal Father, strong to save,
Whose arm hath bound the restless wave,
Who bidd'st the mighty ocean deep
Its own appointed limits keep:
O hear us when we cry to thee
For those in peril on the sea.

2 O Christ, whose voice the waters heard,
And hushed their raging at thy word,
Who walkedst on the foaming deep,
And calm amid the storm didst sleep:
O hear us when we cry to thee
For those in peril on the sea.

3 O Holy Spirit, who didst brood
Upon the waters dark and rude,
And bid their angry tumult cease,
And give, for wild confusion, peace:
O hear us when we cry to thee
For those in peril on the sea.

4 O Trinity of love and power,
Our brethren shield in danger's hour;
From rock and tempest, fire and foe,
Protect them wheresoe'er they go:
Thus evermore shall rise to thee
Glad hymns of praise from land and sea.

The author of this hymn was known to his sixteen
pupils as 'Hoppy' Whiting, on account of his club foot.
He was at that time Master of the Quiristers of Winchester College. By one of life's strange coincidences, a
few years after Whiting's appointment Samuel Sebas-

tian Wesley, Charles Wesley's illegitimate grandson, was appointed Organist of the College. He was also lame, so the boys gave him the same nickname. Thereafter they were known as 'Hoppy' Whiting and 'Hoppy' Wesley.

William Whiting, to give him his correct name, was born in 1825 in Kensington, West London, where his father was a grocer. When he was four years old the family moved to Clapham, then a village on the south side of London. His father's business prospered and as a highly respected church-going family they became friendly with the Rector who was a Prebendary of Winchester; Clapham was then in the diocese of Winchester. When he was sixteen his father died, and the Rector, who was co-founder of Winchester's Training Institution for Schoolmasters, arranged for William to be elected as an Exhibitioner of the Institution. He did well, and was made responsible for the education and upbringing of the sixteen boys, or men as they were traditionally called, in the Quiristers (Choristers) School. A few years later the post of Master was created and William gladly accepted this appointment. He moved into the Quiristers house at 5 College Street, Winchester in 1842 and remained there for the following thirty-six years. He wrote this hymn, frequently referred to as 'The Sailors' Hymn', in 1860. In fact, he produced four versions of the hymn, and when it was first published Whiting appended a note which read, 'For those at sea'. There is also a reasonably founded story that he wrote these lines to comfort one of his pupils about to set sail for America. When it was first published in SPCK's *Psalms and Hymns* it began:

> O thou who bidd'st the ocean deep
> Its own appointed limits keep;
> Thou who dost bind the restless wave,
> Eternal Father, strong to save.

With 'Hoppy' Whiting's approval, when it was included in the first edition of *Hymns Ancient & Modern* (1861), the editors wisely changed the first verse to the present version:

> Eternal Father, strong to save,
> Whose arm hath bound the restless wave,
> Who bidd'st the mighty ocean deep
> Its own appointed limits keep:
> O hear us when we cry to thee
> For those in peril on the sea.

Soon it was adopted by the sailors of the British Empire, subsequently Commonwealth, and even by the French navy *Nouveau Livre Cantique*. When Britain's Prime Minister Winston Churchill met America's President Franklin D. Roosevelt for a secret meeting aboard the warship *Prince of Wales* in the North Atlantic during the Second World War, Churchill chose this hymn for singing at Divisions. And the line 'for those in peril on the sea' was tragically emphasized the following year when the warship was sunk. Of the many Scripture verses reflected in this hymn I mention just one, which it is said was the source of Whiting's inspiration when writing the hymn: 'They that go down to the sea in ships, that do business in great waters; these see the works of the Lord, and his wonders in the deep' (Psalm 107:23, 24 AV).

From heaven you came (the Servant King)

1 From heaven you came, helpless babe,
  Entered our world, your glory veiled,
  Not to be served but to serve,
  And give your life that we might live.
    This is our God, the Servant King,
    He calls us now to follow him,
    To bring our lives as a daily offering
    Of worship to the Servant King.

2 There in the garden of tears
  My heavy load he chose to bear;
  His heart with sorrow was torn,
  'Yet not my will but yours', he said,
    This is our God . . .

3 Come see his hands and his feet,
  The scars that speak of sacrifice,
  Hands that flung stars into space
  To cruel nails surrendered.
    This is our God . . .

4 So let us learn how to serve
  And in our lives enthrone him,
  Each other's needs to prefer,
  For it is Christ we're serving.
    This is our God . . .

This is one of more than 200 hymns by one of today's popular hymn-writers, Graham Kendrick. This word picture of Christ's double role as servant and king seems at first sight to be a contradiction. It is further emphasized by his juxtaposition of a helpless babe whose 'hands . . . flung stars into space'.

> From heav'n you came, helpless babe,
> Enter'd our world, your glory veil'd,
> Not to be served but to serve,
> And give your life that we might live.
> This is our God, the Servant King,
> He calls us now to follow him,
> To bring our lives as a daily offering,
> Of worship to the Servant King.

Our thoughts are then skilfully taken through many facets of the Redeemer's earthly life in the garden of tears and a scarred body on a criminal's Roman cross. His glory was hidden when he came to serve. Then as we proceed through the hymn we are taken to the place where Christ is enthroned in the human heart.

> So let us learn how to serve,
> And in our lives enthrone him;
> Each other's needs to prefer,
> For it is Christ we're serving.

Graham was born on 2nd August 1950 in Blisworth, near Northampton, where his father was pastor of a Baptist church. In subsequent years the family lived in Putney, South London, and Basildon, Essex, where the Revd Mr Kendrick continued his ministry in the Baptist church. Graham chose the teaching profession and enrolled as a student in Avery Hill Training College, Kent. His love of music, coupled with a desire to employ his talents in Christian service, meant that he used all his spare time performing in churches and youth meetings. So it happened that after qualifying as a teacher in 1972 he took a year off to tour schools and colleges with his Christian concert party. This was to set him on a new and unplanned course in life. He had begun to compose his own songs from the time he was fifteen years old, and these he now used for his concerts. Like his illustrious predecessor Isaac Watts, he had started writing because of his dissatisfaction with existing contemporary Christian songs. One day he shared these thoughts with a friend who, like Watts' father, said, 'Go and write something better yourself.'

His compositions spring out of his heart before they emerge through his head, and their emphasis is on praise and worship rather than 'things' to perform. For me they fulfil the qualifications of what Paul calls the gift of prophecy: for the 'strengthening, encouragement and comfort' of Christians (1 Corinthians 14:3 NIV). He told me that his tunes come to him in the same way, as he taps out the melody on his piano which he taught himself to play before he learned to read and write music.

He now lives in South London with his wife and four daughters, and is a member of the Ichthus ministry team led by Roger Forster. The word 'Ichthus' is Greek for a fish (in Christian literature and art this became a symbol of Christ). It is made up of the initial letters of the Greek for 'Jesus Christ, Son of God, Saviour'.

I first encountered Graham's music style around the beginning of the seventies when groups of young people began calling themselves 'Jesus People'. They mainly came from the beaches of California and began wending their way to Calvary Chapel in Costa Mesa (a few miles south of Los Angeles) where an unconventional pastor by the name of Chuck Smith appealed to them. At first the church board objected to these long-haired, bare-footed and guitar-playing hippies walking around the beautifully carpeted sanctuary of this stylish church, which had just been refurbished at great cost. But when Chuck Smith threatened to rip out the carpets the church officers relented. It now has a congregation of 15,000 every Sunday morning, but at the time it numbered about 300. One by one these talented but unusual young people committed their lives and their music to Christ. And the first of their songs to circle the world was Karen Lafferty's 'Seek ye first the Kingdom of God'. They now run the large music division for the church known as Maranatha Music, and it is a place well worth a visit if you are ever in California.

reat is thy faithfulness

1 Great is thy faithfulness, O God my Father,
   There is no shadow of turning with thee;
   Thou changest not, thy compassions they fail not,
   As thou has been thou for ever wilt be.
   Great is thy faithfulness,
   Great is thy faithfulness;
   Morning by morning
   New mercies I see;
   All I have needed
   Thy hand hath provided —
   Great is thy faithfulness,
   Lord, unto me!

2 Summer and winter, and spring-time and harvest,
   Sun, moon and stars in their courses above,
   Join with all nature in manifold witness
   To thy great faithfulness, mercy and love.
   Great is thy faithfulness . . .

3 Pardon for sin, and a peace that endureth,
   Thine own dear presence to cheer and to guide;
   Strength for today and bright hope for tomorrow,
   Blessings all mine, with ten thousand beside!
   Great is thy faithfulness . . .

Two American Methodist ministers gave us the words
and music of this much-loved hymn introduced to most
people in this country by Bev Shea, the Canadian gospel
singer who accompanied Dr Billy Graham when he conducted his first London evangelistic crusade at Harringay in 1954. I well remember his deep melodious bass
voice singing:

Pardon for sin and a peace that endureth,
Thine own dear presence to cheer and to guide:
Strength for today and bright hope for tomorrow,
Blessings all mine, with ten thousand beside.
[*followed by the chorus*]
Great is thy faithfulness! Great is thy faithfulness;
Morning by morning new mercies I see;
All I have needed thy hand hath provided
Great is thy faithfulness, Lord, unto me!

The Revd Thomas Obadiah Chisholm wrote the words.
He was born on 29th July 1866 in a humble log cabin
in Franklin, Kentucky. It is strange that though he only
had an elementary schooling he became a schoolteacher
in his school when he was only sixteen! But in spite of
his limited education he was a success, and by the time
he was twenty-one he had been appointed associate
editor of the weekly newspaper *The Franklin Favourite*.
Six years later, when in his late twenties, he attended
what Americans call a 'revival' meeting which, in Britain, would be a meeting during an evangelistic mission.
The preacher was a Dr H. C. Morrison when Thomas
was converted. Later he joined Dr Morrison's organiz-
ation in Louisville as editor and manager of his publication department. He then felt a call to the ministry
and was ordained in the Methodist Church. He wrote
over 1200 poems, many of which were set to music as
hymns. Although dogged by ill-health from his mid-
forties, which forced him to return to a less arduous life
in business, he lived to an advanced age. He died in
1960. In a letter Thomas wrote in 1941 he describes the
background to this hymn of God's faithfulness as his
personal testimony:

My income has not been large at any time due to
impaired health in the earlier years which has followed me on until now. Although I must not fail to

record here the unfailing faithfulness of a covenant-keeping God and that he has given me many wonderful displays of providing care, for which I am filled with astonishing gratefulness.

It was in 1923 that he sent several of his poems to the editor of an American music publishing company, Hope Publishing Company. He was William Runyan, also a Methodist minister. When William read these verses based on two verses in the third chapter of the book of Lamentations, 'His compassions fail not. They are new every morning: Great is thy faithfulness', he was gripped by them, and later wrote:

This particular poem held such an appeal that I prayed most earnestly that my tune might carry over its message in a worthy way, and the subsequent history of its use indicates that God answered prayer. It was written in Baldwin, Kansas, in 1923 and was first published in my private song pamphlets.

Thomas Chisholm also composed the hymn 'Living for Jesus' which was introduced to this country by Principal George Jeffreys, founder of the Elim Pentecostal Churches, and I first heard it in the 1920s when he came to Swansea to preach to capacity crowds at the old Methodist Central Hall.

Guide me, O thou great Jehovah

1 Guide me, O thou great Jehovah,
  Pilgrim through this barren land;
  I am weak, but thou art mighty;
  Hold me with thy powerful hand:
    Bread of heaven,
  Feed me now and evermore.

2 Open now the crystal fountain,
  Whence the healing stream doth flow;
  Let the fiery, cloudy pillar
  Lead me all my journey through:
    Strong deliverer,
  Be thou still my strength and shield.

.3 When I tread the verge of Jordan,
  Bid my anxious fears subside:
  Death of death, and hell's destruction,
  Land me safe on Canaan's side:
    Songs of praises
  I will ever give to thee.

Two Welshmen combined, quite separately, to give us
this hymn which, for Wales, has become a second
national anthem. One of them was the son of a prosperous farmer in Carmarthenshire who planned to be a
medical doctor. The other was a humble railway worker
from the Rhondda valley. God has no favourites in the
distribution of his talents.

The poet was William Williams of Pantecelyn, who
was affectionately referred to as the 'Sweet Singer of
Wales'. He was converted through the fiery preaching
of the renowned Welsh evangelist, Howel Harris, and

left his medical studies to travel some 95,000 miles over the rolling hills and cloud-swept mountains of his beloved land preaching and singing in spite of being attacked by mobs carrying guns and cudgels. It is no wonder he could write:

> Guide me, O thou great Jehovah,
> Pilgrim through this barren land;
> I am weak, but thou art mighty;
> Hold me with thy powerful hand.

It is said that he wrote the hymn at the request of the Countess of Huntingdon for her 'Young Collegians' of Trefecca College, near Talgarth, mid-Wales. The images of the hymn are basic to life in Wales — mountains, streams, fountains, bread and certainly clouds. It's a prayer for divine guidance during life's pilgrimage and no doubt he had the Israelites also in mind. I have read that he was inspired to write the hymn on a journey across Pen-rhys in the Rhondda in bad weather with the forbidding sight of the mountains shrouded in mist and rain all around him.

William was born at Cefn Coed, Llanfair-ar-y-Bryn, in Carmarthenshire, the son of a prosperous farmer, but when at college in Hay-on-Wye he attended one of Howel Harris's evangelistic meetings which changed the course of his life. At first he thought of becoming a priest in the Anglican church and was ordained deacon by the Bishop of St David's in 1740 and was licensed as a curate of Llanwrtyd, Brecon. This did not last long when he failed to conform to the church's practices because of his evangelical and Calvinistic beliefs. He left the state church to join Howel Harris.

Although he became a well-known preacher it was his hymn-writing that earned him his greatest reputation. He composed 800 hymns in Welsh and 100 in English. This hymn was written in Welsh and translated into English by Peter Williams who also came from Carmarthenshire but they were not related. Peter who was converted through the preaching of George White-field was also ordained as an Anglican deacon and, like William Williams, left to join the Calvinistic Methodists. He translated three of the verses into English. Later William Williams produced his own English version using Peter's translation and adding one of his own. The hymn was first given the title, 'Nerth i fyned trwy'r anialwch' which means 'Strength to pass through the wilderness'.

The tune Cwm Rhondda, which means 'Valley of the babbling stream', was composed by railwayman John Hughes for the annual Salem Baptist Church 'Cymanfa Ganu' (Welsh singing festival) at Llantwit Fardre in 1905. The tune came to him when his minister was preaching one Sunday morning, so there's something to be said for boring sermons! He was born in Dowlais, South Wales, on 22nd November 1873 but moved with his family to Pontypridd the following year. He began his working life as a door-boy at Glyn Colliery when he was only twelve, but later found a better job with the traffic department of the Great Western Railway. He died in Llantwit Fardre on 14th May 1932.

Hold the fort

1 Ho, my comrades! see the signal
Waving in the sky!
Reinforcements now appearing,
Victory is nigh!
    'Hold the fort, for I am coming!'
    Jesus signals still;
    Wave the answer back to heaven,
    'By thy grace we will!'

2 See the mighty host advancing,
Satan leading on:
Mighty men around us falling,
Courage almost gone!

3 See the glorious banner waving!
Hear the trumpet blow!
In our leader's name we'll triumph
Over every foe!

4 Fierce and long the battle rages,
But our help is near;
Onward comes our great Commander,
Cheer, my comrades, cheer!

The writer of this hymn is Philip Paul Bliss who was a well-known author of hymns and composer of tunes in the nineteenth century in North America. He would be inspired on most occasions to write his verses after hearing an illustration used in a sermon.

One day one of the officers serving in the American Civil War called Major W. D. Whittle was speaking to young men at a YMCA meeting when he took this text from the Book of Revelation (2:25); 'But that which you

have already hold fast till I come.' He then told the
story of a small group of Federal soldiers who were
given the responsibility of guarding the quartermaster's
stores at a critical time in the American Civil War. At
this time they were under heavy attack from General
French and the troops of his Confederate Army which
was much larger and stronger. The General called on
this small group of Federal soldiers to surrender, but
just at that moment the Captain of this little band saw
in the distance their commander, General Sherman,
approaching over the horizon with a 'mighty host'. Not
only that but the Captain of the Federal troops also saw
his General's signal with just one short phrase. It simply
said, 'Hold the fort, I am coming. Sherman.' And the
Captain signalled back, 'Sir, we will!' Major Whittle
proudly announced to the young men of the YMCA:
'And they certainly did, with the result that the supplies
and the soldiers were saved.'

As Philip Bliss sat enthralled, listening to Major Whittle's graphic account of that thrilling story, he began to
create his own picture of the event. That night the story
kept running on through his mind and he just could
not get to sleep. Eventually, he rose from his bed and
began to write, 'Ho, my comrades, see the signal
waving in the sky! Reinforcements now appearing, Victory is nigh. "Hold the fort, for I am coming", Jesus
signals still. Wave the answer back to heaven, "By thy
grace we will".' When the meetings at the YMCA were
resumed the next day Philip sat at the piano and played
the tune and sang the words to the delight of his audi-
ence who took it up with enthusiasm as they recalled
Major Whittle's true story. Then followed its adoption
by Moody and Sankey who shortly afterwards brought
it to Britain (1874). Lord Shaftesbury when addressing
the closing meetings of the British mission said: 'If Mr
Sankey has done no more than teach the people to sing
"Hold the Fort", he has conferred inestimable blessing

on the British Empire, and it would have been worth all the expense of these meetings.'

Philip Bliss also wrote such great favourites as 'Brightly beams our Father's mercy'. He was born in a log cabin in the woods of Clearfield County, northern Pennsylvania, on 9th July 1838, the son of a devout Christian and gifted musician. He was only eleven years of age when he was obliged to find work on farms, lumber camps and sawmills. At twelve years he was converted and under the influence of W. B. Bradbury, a music teacher, he took an interest in music. He used to play his melodeon as he trundled his old horse, Fanny, along the country roads. When he was twenty-six he sold his first song to the Chicago publishers, Root and Cady, and shortly afterwards went to work for them.

Although he was not a wealthy man he gave all the royalties from the sale of his music and books to the cause of evangelism, which in the late 1800s amounted to 30,000 dollars. But his end was very sad. He and Mrs Bliss were on a train travelling from the East Coast of America to Chicago when they were involved in a tragic accident. The train caught fire and, though Philip Bliss managed to escape, his wife was trapped by a seat in her carriage. Philip returned to her side and tried to extricate her, but to no avail, and with nearly one hundred other passengers they perished in the fire. It was the night of 29th December 1876.

How great thou art

1 O Lord my God! when I in awesome wonder
  Consider all the works Thy hand hath made,
  I see the stars, I hear the mighty thunder,
  The power throughout the universe displayed;
  Then sings my soul, my Saviour God, to thee,
  How great thou art, how great thou art!
  Then sings my soul, my Saviour God, to thee,
  How great thou art, how great thou art!

2 When through the woods and forest glades I
    wander
  And hear the birds sing sweetly in the trees;
  When I look down from lofty mountain grandeur,
  And hear the brook, and feel the gentle breeze;
  Then sings my soul . . .

3 And when I think that God his Son not sparing,
  Sent him to die — I scarce can take it in,
  That on the cross my burden gladly bearing,
  He bled and died to take away my sin:
  Then sings my soul . . .

4 When Christ shall come with shout of acclamation
  And take me home — what joy shall fill my heart!
  Then shall I bow in humble adoration
  And there proclaim, my God, how great thou art!
  Then sings my soul . . .

One of the many titles that could be given to this hymn
is, 'A hymn for refugees'.

When Stuart Hine returned from the Ukraine at the
outbreak of the Second World War he brought with him
a Swedish song which he had heard sung in the Russian

language. His interest in the land of his adoption did
not diminish during the war years and in 1948, when
there was an influx of displaced persons into Britain
from Eastern Europe, he was deeply moved by these
homeless people. So he thought, 'Where is the real
home for these people?' And that is how the words for
the last verse of this hymn were born. He had previously written the first three verses based on a Swedish
song entitled 'O Store Gud':

When Christ shall come with shout of acclamation,
And take me home, what joy shall fill my heart!
Then shall I bow in humble adoration
And there proclaim, my God, how great thou art!

This hymn, which attracted public attention in 1954
through it being sung by Bev Shea during Billy
Graham's meetings at the Harringay Stadium in
London, came to us by a strange route. Stuart Hine's
English version is based on a poem composed by Carl
Boberg in 1886. He was a man of many parts, a pastor
and evangelist, successful editor and for a time Member
of Parliament. He was born and brought up at Mon-
steras, a beautiful inlet on the south-east coast of
Sweden. He became a Christian when he was nineteen,
and after training for the Christian ministry at the Bible
School at Kristinehamn, he was appointed to the pastorate of a church in his home town. It was there one
summer evening as he gazed upon the rainbow forming
a multi-coloured bridge over the calm waters that the
awesomeness of God as Creator took hold of his
thoughts, which resulted in him writing a poem of nine
verses. Three years later someone set his lines to an old
Swedish melody and found a place for it in some of
Sweden's hymn-books. In the following years it was
translated into several languages including Russian.
This was the version that Stuart Hine heard as a

missionary in the Carpathian mountains as he and his wife worked in the districts surrounding the Russian-Romanian frontiers. Once again the spectacle of God's creative handiwork in this country of breath-taking views inspired Hine to write:

> When through the woods and forest glades I
>   wander
> And hear the birds sing sweetly in the trees,
> When I look down from lofty mountain grandeur
> And hear the brook and feel the gentle breeze,
> Then sings my soul, my Saviour God to thee;
> How great thou art!

For the record it should be said that an American of Swedish descent, Gustav Johnson, literally translated Boberg's hymn into English in 1925 which may be found in some American hymn-books entitled 'O Mighty God, when I behold the wonder', but only the theme bears any similarity to the hymn we know as 'How great thou art'.

Stuart Hine retained the Swedish folk melody and made his own arrangement for his verses.

The Scripture that is most closely aligned to this hymn for me is David's Psalm 19 in the translation by James Moffatt:

> The heavens proclaim God's splendour,
> the sky speaks of his handiwork;
> day after day takes up the tale,
> night after night makes him known;
> their speech has never a word, not a sound for the
>   ear,
> and yet their message spreads the wide world over,
> their meaning carries to earth's end.

I heard the voice of Jesus say

1 I heard the voice of Jesus say,
  'Come unto Me and rest;
  Lay down thou weary one, lay down
  Thy head upon my breast':
  I came to Jesus as I was,
  Weary, and worn, and sad;
  I found in him a resting-place,
  And he has made me glad.

2 I heard the voice of Jesus say,
  'Behold, I freely give
  The living water; thirsty one,
  Stoop down and drink, and live':
  I came to Jesus, and I drank
  Of that life-giving stream;
  My thirst was quenched,
  My soul revived,
  And now I live in him.

3 I heard the voice of Jesus say,
  'I am this dark world's light;
  Look unto me, thy morn shall rise,
  And all thy day be bright':
  I looked to Jesus and I found
  In him my star, my sun;
  And in that light of life I'll walk
  Till travelling days are done.

Hymns have an almost unique ability to cross all denominational barriers. Roman Catholic hymns are sung with enthusiasm in the churches of the Reformation, and I was interested to discover that over forty hymns by the staunch Scottish Calvinist, Dr Horatius

Bonar, can be found in Roman Catholic hymn-books. This hymn was one of the most popular of the people's choice in years gone by, and although it has lapsed in many quarters it has not completely lost its appeal.

It was written in 1846 for the Sunday School children of Leith's Church of Scotland when Horatius was the student-assistant minister. It is based on the words of Jesus in Matthew, 'Come unto me all you that labour and are heavy laden, and I will give you rest' (11:28). Have you noticed that these words of comfort follow the hard words Jesus had spoken (11:20) where he denounced the apathy of the crowds? He reserves his words of comfort for simple men of understanding who receive his message with childlike faith.

To be simple does not mean one has to be without intellectual ability because Dr Bonar was an eminent theologian and a student of Greek and Latin classics. Although he appeared to be austere he had a warm heart for the children of his parish. In fact, it was because he was aware that the metrical versions of the Scottish psalms failed to attract his young people's interest that he decided to turn his attention to hymn-writing. This was to earn him the title of 'Prince of Scottish hymn-writers' with more than 600 hymns to his credit. It was his custom to jot down his ideas and phrases as they came to him on his country walks, which is how this hymn came to be written. After his death his son found a faded pencil copy of his original writing and this is now included in the son's collection of Dr Bonar's hymns published in 1905.

Horatius Bonar was born in Edinburgh on 19th December 1808, the son of a Solicitor for Excise for Scotland. After reading Divinity at university under Dr Thomas Chalmers he was licensed to preach in the Church of Scotland where he was ordained minister of the North Parish of Kelso on 30th November 1837. However, along with other prominent ministers, including his Professor, Dr Chalmers, he left to found the Free Church of Scotland. After twenty-seven years of ministry at Kelso he moved to the Chalmers Memorial Church in Edinburgh and was made Moderator of the General Assembly in 1883. He died six years later.

Two tunes are usually used with Dr Bonar's words. *'Vox Dilecti'*, by John Bacchus Dykes, and 'Kingsfold', a Sussex County folk-song adapted and arranged by Ralph Vaughan Williams.

Kingsfold is a village on the Sussex-Surrey borders half way between Horsham and Dorking, and two miles from the house where Vaughan Williams lived at Leith Hill. It was in the village of Kingsfold that Vaughan Williams heard the tune which he used in a fantasia for strings and harp, giving it the name of the village. Also living in the district was Lucy Broadwood, of the piano family, whose hobby was to collect English county songs and this folk melody is included in one of her publications in 1893. The tune is also known as 'The Star of the County Down' and some hymnologists believe its origin goes back to the Middle Ages both in Ireland and the south-east of England when travellers in commerce visited one another's countries.

In Christ there is no East or West

1 In Christ there is no East or West,
   In him no South or North,
   But one great fellowship of love
   Throughout the whole wide earth.

2 In him shall true hearts everywhere
   Their high communion find:
   His service is the golden cord
   Close-binding all mankind.

3 Join hands then, brothers of the faith,
   Whate'er your race may be!
   Who serves my Father as a son
   Is surely kin to me.

4 In Christ now meet both East and West,
   In him meet South and North,
   All Christly souls are one in him,
   Throughout the whole wide earth.

In 1908 the London Missionary Society, the overseas missions arm of the Congregational Church of England and Wales, hired the cavernous Agricultural Hall in London to present their month-long missionary pageant produced by the Revd Dugald Macfadyen. He was the nephew of the author of this hymn. In our hymn-books his name is given as John Oxenham, but this was only his pen-name. He was William Arthur Dunkerley, a deacon of the Ealing Congregational Church, London, a journalist, poet and editor, who found his writing was so successful that he devoted the whole of his life to it. He was born in Cheetham,

Manchester, on 12th November 1852, and following his education at Victoria University, Manchester, entered the family business of wholesale provisions. He spent five years in France after which he married and crossed the Atlantic to New York to set up a branch of the family business. Whilst there his literary skills came to the fore and by 1881 he had returned to England to open an office for the *Detroit Free Press* and to launch the magazines *The Idler* and *Today*. His partner in this enterprise was no less a person than the author of *Three Men in a Boat*, Jerome K. Jerome. As a sideline he did some writing privately which proved to be so successful that he left his American publishers, set up home in Hanger Hill Farm in Ealing, and for his writings adopted the name of Charles Kingsley's seadog in *Westward Ho!*, John Oxenham. Apparently it was his Sunday School teacher who had given him a copy of Kingsley's book, and he was so successful in hiding his true identity under this pseudonym that even his close friends were not aware of it. As a past publisher I was amused to discover that Dunkerley failed to find a publisher for a book he wrote in 1913, *Bees in Amber*, so he published it himself and sold 286,000 copies! In all he wrote forty novels but also found time to conduct a Bible class each Sunday at his church in Ealing. He retired to High Salvington, Worthing, where he died on 23rd January 1941.

He wrote the words of this hymn as part of the libretto for music by Hamish MacCunn entitled 'The Pageant of Darkness and Light' at the request of his nephew. 'In Christ there is no east or west' is based on the words of Paul in Galatians 3:28, 'There is neither Jew nor Greek, there is neither bond nor free, there is neither male nor female: for ye are all one in Christ Jesus'; and the words of Jesus in Matthew 8:11, 'And I say unto you, That many shall come from the east and west, and shall sit down with Abraham, and Isaac, and Jacob, in the kingdom of heaven.'

The hymn is a fine expression of the unity there is in Christ, not only in our evangelistic enterprises abroad, for which the London Missionary Society and similar organizations were formed, but the unity which transcends all earthly divisions racial or doctrinal.

It is most often sung to the tune 'McKee' which has a very interesting history. It is an adaptation of the melody of the Negro spiritual 'I know the angels done changed my name', which was in the famous *Jubilee Songs* of 1884 published by the Negro college, Fisk University. But, according to C. V. Stanford, it began its life in Ireland and was taken to the USA by emigrants and adopted by the Negro slaves. This arrangement was made by H. T. Burleigh for *The Hymnal* in 1940 where it was first set to these words, and named after the Rev. Elmer M. McKee, who was rector of St George's Church, New York.

In the bleak mid-winter

1 In the bleak mid-winter,
   Frosty wind made moan,
   Earth stood hard as iron,
   Water like a stone;
   Snow had fallen, snow on snow,
   Snow on snow,
   In the bleak mid-winter,
   Long ago.

2 Our God, heaven cannot hold him,
   Nor earth sustain,
   Heaven and earth shall flee away
   When he comes to reign;
   In the bleak mid-winter
   A stable-place sufficed
   The Lord God almighty,
   Jesus Christ.

3 Angels and archangels
   May have gathered there,
   Cherubim and seraphim
   Thronged the air;
   But his mother only,
   In her maiden bliss,
   Worshipped the beloved
   With a kiss.

4 What can I give him,
   Poor as I am?
   If I were a shepherd,
   I would bring a lamb;
   If I were a wise man,
   I would do my part;

Yet what I can I give him —
Give my heart.

This was written as a poem rather than a hymn in
the year 1870, and one can imagine that with such
descriptive words as,

> Frosty wind made moan,
> Earth stood hard as iron,
> Water like a stone.

This vividly imaginative expression of the events surrounding the birth of Jesus was very much in line with
the character of the lady who wrote the words. She
was Christina Georgina Rossetti, born in St Pancras,
London, on 5th December 1830, the daughter of Professor Gabriele Rossetti, an Italian refugee. Her brother
was William Michael Rossetti one of the founders of the
magazine of the Pre-Raphaelites, *The Germ*. In fact,
some of Christina's early works of poetry as a child
were published in this magazine.

When Christina walked into a room heads would
turn to watch this strikingly beautiful woman. She was
frequently sought after by many artists as a model for
their paintings, including Holman Hunt. She was
intensely religious, a devout Anglican, which helped
her endure her suffering from illness in later life, and
also the sacrifice she made of the one person she would
have married, James Collinson, one of the pre-Raphael-
ite Brotherhood. In fact they became engaged to marry
on the understanding that he would leave the Church
of Rome. Although he kept to his word he later felt
compelled to rejoin the Roman Catholic Church and, as
Christina's convictions were also strong and meant that
she could not agree to any children of the marriage
being raised as Catholics, their engagement was

broken, and this hurt her deeply. She remained single for the remainder of her life, which ended peacefully in London on 29th December 1894.

Walter de la Mare described her poems as 'numinous', that is, spiritually inspired. These simple lines have a deeply penetrating quality about them which cannot be sung lightly:

What can I give him, poor as I am?
If I were a shepherd I would bring a lamb;
If I were a wise man I would do my part;
Yet what I can, I give him — give my heart.

The following verse was included in her original poem but omitted from most hymn-books:

Enough for him, whom cherubim
Worship night and day,
A breastful of milk,
And a mangerful of hay:
Enough for him, whom angels
Fall down before,
The ox and ass and camel
Which adore.

Gustav Holst composed the tune 'Cranham' named after his birthplace near Cheltenham, especially for Christina's hymn. It was first published in the *English Hymnal* in 1906. Holst was born on 21st September 1874, the great grandson of an *émigré* from Sweden. Early in his life he was plagued by neuritis which interfered with his career as a concert pianist, so when he was seventeen he turned to the organ. Although he continued to suffer considerable pain from his affliction, and was surprisingly somewhat over-sensitive to criticism, he won fame from his compositions and the teaching of composition at the Royal College of Music.

However, the hymn 'In the bleak mid-winter' was given a new lease of life in the 'sixties when Sir David Willcocks included it, set to the music of Harold Darke, in the BBC's Christmas Eve broadcast from King's College Chapel, Cambridge. It soon became a national favourite. Dr Darke, who composed the tune in 1911, was born in Highbury, London, in 1888, and educated at the Royal College of Music where he won the Tagore Gold Medal. After many distinguished organ appointments he joined the staff of the Royal College of Music and in 1925 founded the City of London Choral Union.

Jerusalem the golden

1 Jerusalem the golden,
   With milk and honey blest,
   Beneath thy contemplation
   Sink heart and voice oppressed:
   I know not, O I know not
   What social joys are there,
   What radiancy of glory,
   What light beyond compare.

2 They stand, those halls of Zion,
   Conjubilant with song,
   And bright with many an angel,
   And all the martyr throng:
   The Prince is ever in them;
   The daylight is serene;
   The pastures of the blessed
   Are decked in glorious sheen.

3 There is the throne of David,
   And there, from care released,
   The shout of them that triumph,
   The song of them that feast;
   And they who, with their Leader,
   Have conquered in the fight,
   For ever and for ever
   Are clad in robes of white.

4 O sweet and blessed country,
   The home of God's elect!
   O sweet and blessed country,
   That eager hearts expect!
     Jesus, in mercy bring us
     To that dear land of rest,

Who art, with God the Father
And Spirit, ever blest. Amen.

I wonder how many brides singing this hymn in their
bridal gowns are aware of its colourful origin.

It was not written as a hymn, but as a satirical poem
on the lifestyles of the monks of Cluny, in France, in
the early part of the twelfth century, and the author was
a humble monk we now know as Bernard of Morlaix.
In fact, although he was born in Morlaix in Bretagne
(Brittany) his parents were English.

Bernard entered the Abbey of Cluny between 1122
and 1156 when Peter the Venerable was the Abbot and
it was during this time that Bernard composed this
poem which he called *De Contemptu Mundi* ('Of Scorn-
ing the World'). A copy is held in the Bodleian Library,
Oxford. It consists of 2966 lines in dactylic hexameter;
these are lines divided into three sections by internal
rhymes and linked in pairs by terminal rhymes. The
composition of such an intricate rhyme-scheme of such
tremendous length called for all the poet's power.
When Bernard completed writing the poem in 1145 he
said: 'Unless the Spirit of wisdom and understanding
had flowed in upon me, I could not have put together
so long a work in so difficult a metre.'

The reason for him writing this satire about the Abbey
of Cluny was because it was renowned throughout
Europe for its opulence and gross self-indulgence. The
buildings, now in ruins, were also strikingly beautiful
and the most magnificent in France. The extravagant
lifestyle of the monks of the Abbey did not fit into the
thinking of this humble monk. This is how he described
the lengths to which the Abbey's chefs went in the
preparation of an egg just to gratify the taste buds of
these 'holy men' and their guests:

Who could say in how many ways eggs are cooked
and worked up? With what care they are turned in
and out, made hard or soft, or chopped fine; now
fried, now roasted, now stuffed! Even the external
appearance of the dishes is such that the eye, as
well as the taste, is charmed, and when the stomach
complains that it is full, curiosity is still alive.

In the poem Bernard compared the tinsel of the self-
indulgent and earthly Cluny with the eternal glory of
the New Jerusalem as described in the Book of Revelation. In 1858, 700 years after Bernard wrote this enormous poem, the eccentric Anglican scholar and priest
of East Grinstead in Sussex, John Mason Neale, translated 218 lines and published it under the title *The
rhythm of Bernard De Morlaix, Monk of Cluny, on the Cel-
estial Country*. He was the first to translate any part of
the poem and wisely chose the section which contained
a simple ballad rhythm. It is through his brilliant trans-
lating skills that we have this magnificent hymn which
came from the lines beginning 'Urbs Sion Aurea'. It is
almost ironic that this part of St Bernard's poem has
become the favourite of brides for their wedding day
while they remain blissfully unaware of its satirical
character.

Dr Neale in his comments on the poem wrote:

The great part is a bitter satire on the fearful corrup-
tions of the age. But as a contrast to the misery and
pollution of earth, the poem opens with a description
of the peace and glory of heaven, of such rare beauty
as not easily to be matched by any mediaeval composition on the same subject.

The hymn draws heavily on biblical imagery, especially
in the Book of Revelation, with a picture of the New
Jerusalem and the River of the Water of Life. The last

verse expresses the Christian's longing for the satisfying
nature of the Eternal City which is beyond comparison
with the tawdry nature of the man-made Abbey.

Jesus, lover of my soul

1 Jesus, lover of my soul,
   Let me to thy bosom fly,
   While the nearer waters roll,
   While the tempest still is high:
   Hide me, O my Saviour, hide,
   Till the storm of life is past;
   Safe into the haven guide;
   O receive my soul at last!

2 Other refuge have I none,
   Hangs my helpless soul on thee;
   Leave, ah! leave me not alone,
   Still support and comfort me:
   All my trust on thee is stayed;
   All my help from thee I bring;
   Cover my defenceless head
   With the shadow of thy wing.

3 Thou, O Christ, art all I want;
   More than all in thee I find;
   Raise the fallen, cheer the faint,
   Heal the sick, and lead the blind.
   Just and holy is thy name,
   I am all unrighteousness;
   False, and full of sin I am,
   Thou art full of truth and grace.

4 Plenteous grace with thee is found,
   Grace to cover all my sin;
   Let the healing streams abound,
   Make and keep me pure within.
   Thou of life the fountain art,
   Freely let me take of thee;

Spring thou up within my heart,
Rise to all eternity.

This would have to be a hymn, with the tune 'Aberystwyth', I would have to take with me for my sojourn on
my desert island. Not only for its emotional associations
with Wales, but because of its perfectly formed
expression of love for the world's Saviour.

As with many other hymns several stories are given
as the background to the writing of this hymn by
Charles Wesley, Susanna Wesley's eighteenth child,
she having been one of a family of twenty-five. Very
large families, even without the Pope's influence, seem
to have been commonplace in those days! The most
reasonable explanation of this hymn of Charles Wesley
for me is that it describes not his conversion experience
but what the old Wesleyans and some of the Keswick
teachers used to call his 'second blessing'. It was written
a year after Charles had undergone a deep spiritual
experience which, I have to admit, the majority of his
biographers describe as his conversion. The more I have
read both their writings and the relevant parts of Wesley's journals I am inclined to the view that he was
already a Christian at this time.

This hymn contains three deeply felt experiences
which touched the core of Charles Wesley's life around
this time.

The first was when he was on board ship crossing
the Atlantic as he was returning from Georgia, USA, to
England in the autumn of 1736. Both the Wesley
brothers had previously left England to join the staff
of General Oglethorpe, the Governor of Georgia, with
Charles acting as his secretary. This was not a success
so they soon made their way back home. During that
sea journey there was a horrendous storm which
Charles wrote about in his journal:

Thurs. Oct. 28: The captain warned me of a storm approaching. In the evening at eight it came, and rose higher and higher . . . The sea streamed in at the sides so plentifully that it was as much as four men could do by continual pumping to keep her above water. I rose and lay down by turns, but could remain in no posture long; strove vehemently to pray, but in vain. I prayed for . . . faith in Jesus Christ continually repeating his name . . . In this dreadful moment, I bless God, I found comfort of hope . . . I went to Mr Brig and Mr Cutler and endeavoured from their fear to show them the want of religion . . . if God saved them from this distress, that they would instantly and entirely give themselves up to him. . . . Toward morning the sea heard and obeyed the divine voice, 'Peace, be still'.

Friday, Dec. 3. At six the pilot came on board. In half an hour we reached the shore. I knelt down and blessed the 'hand' that has conducted me through such inextricable mazes.

With those words and that incident in mind consider these lines,

> Jesus, lover of my soul,
> Let me to thy bosom fly,
> While the nearer waters roll,
> While the tempest still is high;
> Hide me, O my Saviour, hide,
> Till the storm of life is past;
> Safe into the haven guide;
> O receive my soul at last.

The second experience was almost an uncanny one. It was Whit Sunday of 1738 (21st May) and Charles was ill in the grip of an intermittent fever, complicated by pleurisy and dysentery. He was staying in the home of a Mr Bray who according to Charles Wesley was 'a poor innocent mechanic who knows nothing but Christ'. Wesley was in bed upstairs praying for the gift of the Holy Spirit when he heard a voice say, 'In the name of Jesus of Nazareth, arise and believe, and thou shalt be healed of thine infirmities.' Quite astonished Charles sat up in bed, took up his Bible which fell open at the words of David in Psalm 40 and he read: 'And he hath put a new song in my mouth, even praise unto our God.' He rose from his bed, dressed and went downstairs to discover that Mr Bray's sister shyly confessed that she had said the words he thought had come from heaven or some such place. Charles later recorded in his journal: 'I now found myself at peace with God . . .' John Wesley later said of his brother's recovery, 'His bodily strength returned also from that hour.' This event is reflected in the verse,

> Thou, O Christ, art all I want;
> More than all in thee I find;
> Raise the fallen, cheer the faint,
> Heal the sick, and lead the blind.

Just under two months later (apparently in the week beginning 12th July 1738) he was deeply moved by a visit to London's Newgate prison and the fact that ten of the prisoners were hanged on Tyburn Hill. Here are some notes from his journal:

> July 12: Preached at Newgate to the condemned felons, and visited one of them in his cell, sick of fever — a poor black that had robbed his master. I told him of One who came down from heaven to save lost sinners. [With tears the man asked John] 'What! Was it for me? Did God suffer all this for so poor a creature as me?'
> July 17: At Newgate I preached on death (which

they must suffer the day after tomorrow). . . . The black was quite happy.

July 18: I administered the sacrament to the black, and eight more; having first instructed them in the nature of it.

July 19: I rose very heavy, to visit them for the last time. At six I prayed and sang with them all together. All the ten received (the sacrament). At half-hour past nine their irons were knocked off and their hands tied. I went in a coach. . . . The black had spied me coming out of the coach, and saluted me with his looks. As often as his eyes met mine, he smiled with the most composed, delightful countenance I ever saw.

This event had such a profound effect on Wesley, that he wrote,

> Plenteous grace with thee is found,
> Grace to cover all my sin;
> [*and*]
> Spring thou up within my heart,
> Rise to all eternity.

Charles Wesley gave this very moving hymn the title: 'In time of prayer and temptation'.

Apparently John Wesley was embarrassed by his brother's use of the word 'Lover' which, according to some hymnologists, accounts for the exclusion of the hymn from John's original collection of hymns. However, this was rectified in 1780.

The tune 'Aberystwyth' is named after the University College of Wales on the west coast where the author Joseph Parry was Professor of Music. He was born in Cyfarthfa, Merthyr Tydfil, in May 1841 into a very poor Welsh family. In fact, by the time he was ten he was working in the steel furnaces in the local works. Three years later his parents left for America and a new life for their children and settled in Danville, Pennsylvania. Joseph was taught music in Pennsylvania in a class conducted by fellow-Welshmen little realizing it would take him back to Wales as a teacher. His workmates clubbed together to raise the funds necessary to send him to one of New York's music colleges. The following year (1862) he returned to Wales and here again friends contributed to the cost of his studies at the Royal Academy of Music. Parry set Wesley's words to a tune from his cantata *Ceridwen* (a somewhat startling conclusion to a Druidical tale). I like Professor Wesley Milgate's advice to choir conductors: 'The tune, "Aberystwyth", must move, but not too fast, and with some massiveness.'

Jesus, thou joy of loving hearts

1 Jesus, thou Joy of loving hearts,
  Thou Fount of life, thou Light of men,
  From the best bliss that earth imparts
  We turn unfilled to thee again.

2 Thy truth unchanged hath ever stood;
  Thou savest those that on thee call:
  To them that seek thee thou art good,
  To them that find thee, all in all.

3 We taste thee, O thou living Bread,
  And long to feast upon thee still;
  We drink of thee, the Fountain-head,
  And thirst our souls from thee to fill.

4 Our restless spirits yearn for thee,
  Where'er our changeful lot is cast —
  Glad when thy gracious smile we see,
  Blest when our faith can hold thee fast.

5 O Jesus, ever with us stay;
  Make all our moments calm and bright;
  Chase the dark night of sin away;
  Shed o'er the world thy holy light.

As I was in my study in the village of Whyteleafe preparing my radio programme, *Morning Has Broken*, the telephone rang. A voice, very weak and difficult to hear, said: 'Speak to me Jack, I'm in terrible pain.' Then I recognized the voice. It was Raja, my Sri Lankan friend, and a regular listener to my Sunday morning broadcasts on Radio 4, who was dying suffering from a cancerous growth in his spine. Drugs had failed to deaden that pain. I quickly took the train to his home in Croydon and found him writhing on his bed in excruciating agony. What could I do?

When the telephone rang and I heard dear Raja's weak voice I was reading the background to this hymn, which we believe was written by the saintly Bernard of Clairvaux, and I felt the best I could do was to read, very quietly, these words to my dying friend:

> Thy truth unchanged hath ever stood,
> Thou savest those that on thee call;
> To them that seek thee thou art good,
> To them that find thee all in all.

Bernard was a man of noble birth who became a monk and a writer of hymns. When he was young he was not averse to writing some rude verses, but like Francis of Assisi when he looked into the blue eyes of the Nazarene, he was only too willing to abandon his dissolute life and devote himself to his Lord. He entered the Cistercian monastery at Cîteaux in AD 1113 and shortly afterwards founded the community at Clairvaux where he remained for the rest of his life. Luther said that Bernard was the best monk who ever lived. He was born in his father's castle at Les Fontaines near the delightful city of Dijon where I have enjoyed many an overnight stay *en route* for the south. Once he had been faced with the challenge of Christ this very good-looking French nobleman was prepared to renounce the privileges of his birth, his considerable wealth and his most comfortable lifestyle to don the habit of a humble monk for a celibate life of simplicity and spiritual contemplation. One day this elegant, golden-haired young man was riding to join the Duke of Burgundy's army when he unexpectedly heard the voice of God calling him. It had such a profound effect on him that he abandoned his colourful career to become a monk, with such an effect on his family that his uncle and two brothers also left all to join him. Though he was to win fame as an eloquent preacher, who could command the obedience of kings, he preferred worshipping Christ in a primitive cell.

In 1858 Ray Palmer, an American Congregational minister, translated and paraphrased part of his poem, now in the Bodleian Library, Oxford, to give us this most moving devotional hymn,

> Jesus, thou joy of loving hearts,
> Thou fount of life, thou light of men;
> From the best bliss that earth imparts
> We turn unfilled to thee again.

Dr Palmer was born in Little Compton, Rhode Island on 12th November 1808 the son of a judge. For some unknown reason he chose to spend his early life working in a department store but it resulted in his personal commitment to Christ and joining the Park Street Congregation Church, New York. Later he returned to university to read theology and was subsequently ordained in 1835.

Joy to the world

1 Joy to the world, the Lord has come!
  Let earth receive her King;
  Let every heart prepare him room
     And heaven and nature sing,
     And heaven and nature sing,
     And heaven, and heaven and nature sing!

2 Joy to the earth, the Saviour reigns!
  Your sweetest songs employ
  While fields and streams and hills and plains
     Repeat the sounding joy,
     Repeat the sounding joy,
     Repeat, repeat the sounding joy.

3 He rules the world with truth and grace,
  And makes the nations prove –
  The glories of his righteousness,
     The wonders of his love,
     The wonders of his love,
     The wonders, wonders of his love.

Christmas would not be Christmas without Handel's *Messiah*. But if it had not been for a button on his coat we would not have had his immortal oratorio, from which the tune for Isaac Watts' 'Joy to the world' is said to have been derived.

When Handel was a young man he frequently worked with his friend the distinguished composer, musician and conductor, Matheson. One day they were together in Hamburg to perform Matheson's opera *Cleopatra*. Matheson had left the conductor's seat to sing the part of Anthony on stage (he was also a fine soloist), and handed his baton to Handel. However, when

Matheson returned to take the conductor's seat Handel
refused to give it up to him! So, the enraged Matheson
challenged Handel to a duel, and they promptly left
the theatre for the square outside and drew swords.
Matheson lunged with his sword straight for Handel's
heart as the crowds of theatre-goers gasped in horror.
Miraculously, a large button on Handel's coat deflected
the point of the sword and saved the young man's life.
So, but for a large button on Handel's coat the world
would not have had the glorious music of *Messiah*! The
reason why the name 'Antioch' was given to this tune
is unknown but it may have been because that is where
Christ's followers were first called Christian. Antioch
was also the place where some believe that St Ignatius
taught Christians antiphonal singing.

When Isaac Watts wrote, 'Joy to the world, the Lord
is come!' he really rose to the challenge of his father to
write brighter hymns for the people to sing. It is one of
the most joyous Christmas hymns, not in the sense of
merrymaking but in the deep realization of what
Christ's birth has meant to mankind. He based his
verses on these glorious words from an unknown
author:

> Make a joyful noise unto the Lord, all the earth: make
> a loud noise, and rejoice, and sing praise. Sing unto
> the Lord with the harp; with the harp, and the voice
> of a psalm, with trumpets and sound of cornet make
> a joyful noise before the Lord, the King. Let the sea
> roar, and the fulness thereof; the world, and they
> that dwell therein. Let the floods clap their hands:
> let the hills be joyful together before the Lord; for he
> cometh to judge the earth: with righteousness shall
> he judge the world, and the people with equity
> (Psalm 98:4–9).

3333333

And Watts gave the hymn the title, 'The Messiah's Coming and Kingdom'.

He turned this magnificent old Jewish psalm into a Christian song of rejoicing, a Christmas carol, if you like, and gave these great expressions of the past a fresh interpretation. The psalmist calls on the whole earth as one enormous orchestra to make a joyful noise unto the Lord and make known the coming of the Lord's salvation. Many hymnologists place it on a level with the universally used doxology, 'Praise God from whom all blessings flow'. Watts published his hymn in *The Psalms of David* in 1719.

Just as I am

1 Just as I am, without one plea,
But that thy blood was shed for me,
And that thou bidd'st me come to thee,
O Lamb of God, I come!

2 Just as I am, and waiting not
To rid my soul of one dark blot,
To thee, whose blood can cleanse each spot
O Lamb of God, I come!

3 Just as I am, though tossed about
With many a conflict, many a doubt,
Fightings and fears within, without,
O Lamb of God, I come!

4 Just as I am, poor wretched, blind;
Sight, riches, healing of the mind,
Yea, all I need in thee to find,
O Lamb of God, I come!

5 Just as I am, thou wilt receive,
Wilt welcome, pardon, cleanse, relieve:
Because thy promise I believe,
O Lamb of God, I come!

6 Just as I am, thy love unknown
Hath broken every barrier down;
Now, to be thine, yea thine alone,
O Lamb of God, I come!

This hymn has been heard and sung by countless millions of people through the televising of Billy Graham's evangelistic meetings throughout the world. I was co-chairman of the counselling and follow-up programme when Billy was in London in the 'sixties, and I don't remember one meeting when this hymn was not used. This is all the more remarkable when you know how this hymn came to be written.

Charlotte Elliott was born in 1789, the daughter of the vicar of Clapham, south London, and the grand-daughter of Revd Henry Venn, one of the Clapham sect led by William Wilberforce. Her home was a thorough-fare for the famous personalities of the day, but when she was thirty-two years old she was stricken with an illness that left her a semi-invalid. Now unable to take much part in the 'goings-on' she quickly became embitt-ered, having to be confined for the most time to her bedroom. But one day one of these illustrious visitors, a Dr César Malan of Switzerland, came to the vicarage and noticing her sadness took her aside and gently asked if she had ever thought of taking her troubles to Jesus. She was hurt and affronted, and was not slow to show it. After all, her father was the vicar, a good evangelical parson.

The gentle Swiss minister quietly accepted Charlotte's reproof and withdrew. However, before Dr Malan left she sought him out and apologized for her behaviour, adding, 'but I just don't know how to come to Jesus'. He replied with words like: 'Come just as you are.'

It was twelve years later and the Elliott household had moved to the Sussex coastal resort of Brighton where Charlotte's brother, Harry, was also a vicar. Charlotte was living with her brother but again confined to her sickroom feeling utterly useless because she was unable to assist his fund-raising programme to build a school for the education of the daughters of poor clergy. She had already written many poems, and thinking of how she could help from her room decided to write a hymn. It was then that she remembered Dr Malan's words in the context of the words of Jesus, 'Him that cometh unto me, I will in no wise cast out' (John 6:37). These thoughts coupled with her enriched spiritual existence and the strength and peace she now enjoyed, she picked up her pen and began to write: 'Just as I am, without one plea but that thy blood was shed for me, and that thou bidd'st me to come to thee, O Lamb of God, I come.'

She wrote six verses which were published in 1836 in the *Invalid's Hymn Book*, and shortly afterwards wrote the seventh which was published in her book *House of Sorrow Cheered and Comforted*. All the royalties of the hymn were donated to her brother's school for the daughters of impoverished clergy.

Of the seven verses I think that this next verse most clearly expresses her frame of mind at the time of her conversion: 'Just as I am, though tossed about with many a conflict, many a doubt, fightings and fears within, without, O Lamb of God, I come.'

The above story took place between 160 and 170 years ago. But now come with me to a small town in the Midwest of the USA in the year 1937. Another evangelist by the name of Mordecai Hamm had just concluded his evangelistic appeal and invited people to 'get out of their seats and walk to the front' as an act of commitment to Christ. He invited the congregation to sing Charlotte's hymn as the converts walked forward.

In that meeting a young man in his late teens wrestled with the invitation to follow Christ until the final verse, and then he responded as they sang, 'Now to be thine, yea, thine alone, O Lamb of God, I come.'

That young man was Billy Graham!

This is a story of encouragement for the unseen writer. How was Charlotte Elliott to know that the words she wrote in Brighton many years earlier would have a part in the conversion of a young man who was to become probably the greatest evangelist of all time, and at whose meetings many millions have also sung

Charlotte's words: 'Just as I am — thy love unknown hath broken every barrier down — now to be thine, yea, thine alone, O Lamb of God, I come.'

Lead kindly Light

1 Lead kindly Light, amid the encircling gloom,
  Lead thou me on;
  The night is dark, and I am far from home;
  Lead thou me on.
  Keep thou my feet; I do not ask to see
  The distant scene; one step enough for me.

2 I was not ever thus, nor prayed that thou
  Shouldst lead me on;
  I loved to choose and see my path; but now
  Lead thou me on.
  I loved the garish day, and, spite of fears,
  Pride ruled my will: remember not past years.

3 So long thy power has blest me, sure it still
  Will lead me on
  O'er moor and fen, o'er crag and torrent, till
  The night is gone;
  And with the morn those angel faces smile
  Which I have loved long since, and lost awhile.

I never felt attracted to this hymn until I found out how
it came to be written. Just as two people looking at the
same picture will see different things, I thought that
this hymn was too depressing to sing.

And this is how the hymn came to be written. The
year was 1833 and John Henry Newman, the author,
had been in Italy for the sake of his health, but he was
also restless, worrying about the spiritual decline of the
Church of England. 'I began to think I had a mission',
he said. One night he was so ill Gennaro, his faithful
Italian servant, thought he was dying. 'I shall not die,
Gennaro,' Newman said, 'I have not sinned against

light. God has a work for me to do in England. . . .'
Though later he admitted he did not know quite what
he meant by that.

It was midsummer and he was in Sicily at the time
and though he was dreadfully sick he decided to make
his way to Palermo. When he had been in Rome he had
had conversations with Monsignor Wiseman, Rector of
the English College of the Roman Catholic Church. He
was attracted to Rome but still uneasy about its doc-
trines. He had entered Oriel College, Oxford, as an
evangelical but soon he was attracted to the teachings
of John Keble and the influence of his High Church
contemporaries.

He decided that he had stayed long enough in Italy.
Finding a berth in an orange boat at Palermo, which
was bound for Marseilles, he began his journey home.
Before he set sail he summed up the conflict raging
inside his mind in these significant lines:

Oh, that thy creed were sound!
For thou dost soothe the heart,
Thou Church of Rome.
There on a foreign shore
The homesick solitary finds a friend.
Thoughts, prisoned long for lack of speech, outpour
Their tears; and doubts in resignation end.
I almost fainted from the long delay
That tangles me within this languid bay,
When comes a foe, my wounds with oil and wine to
tend!

But in the Straits of Bonifacio between the islands of
Sardinia and Corsica his ship was becalmed, which
meant that with time on his hands he could reflect more
deeply on the state of the Church that would face him
on his return to Oxford. Though he may not then have
contemplated leaving the Church of England I believe

the die was cast in the stillness of the becalmed orange boat almost motionless on the Mediterranean sea. As he knelt in his cabin the story of Moses and the Israelites being guided by the pillar of cloud through the uncharted wastes of the wilderness (Exodus 13:21, 22) came to his mind, and taking his pen he began to write:

> Lead kindly light, amid the encircling gloom,
> Lead thou me on;
> The night is dark, and I am far from home,
> Lead thou me on.
> Keep thou my feet; I do not ask to see
> The distant scene; one step enough for me.

Newman arrived back in Oxford in July 1833 in time to greet the Revd John Keble in the pulpit of his own church at St Mary's, and hear Keble preach his memorable Assize sermon on 'National Apostasy' that was to mark the beginning of the Oxford Movement with Newman as its chief propagandist. The following year Newman's hymn was published in the *British Magazine* under the title 'The Pillar of Cloud'.

For the following twelve years Newman worked hard writing and distributing his *Tracts for the Times* (hence the name Tractarians), endeavouring to prevent the rise of rationalism and liberalism in the Anglican Church. This is often overlooked by evangelicals today. In the end he gave up the struggle and to the horror of his friends, and even John Keble, he left 'England' to join 'Rome'.

He founded the Order of St Philip Neri, of the sixteenth century, in Birmingham, becoming Father Superior, and in 1879 the Pope made him a Cardinal.

He was born in the heart of London's West End, Old Bond Street, on 21st February 1801, the son of a city banker. He died in his Birmingham Oratory at Edgbaston on 11th August 1890.

Leave it there

1 If the world from you withhold of its silver and its
      gold,
  And you have to get along with meagre fare,
  Just remember, in his Word,
  How he feeds the little bird —
  Take your burden to the Lord and leave it there.
      Leave it there, leave it there,
      Leave it there, leave it there,
      Take your burden to the Lord and leave it there;
          leave it there;
      If you trust and never doubt,
      He will surely bring you out —
      Take your burden to the Lord and leave it there.

2 If your body suffers pain and your health you can't
      regain,
  And your soul is almost sinking in despair,
  Jesus knows the pain you feel,
  He can save and he can heal —
  Take your burden to the Lord and leave it there.

3 When your enemies assail and your heart begins to
      fail,
  Don't forget that God in heaven answers prayer;
  He will make a way for you
  And will lead you safely through —
  Take your burden to the Lord and leave it there.

4 When your youthful days are gone and old age is
      stealing on,
  And your body bends beneath the weight of care,
  He will never leave you then,
  He'll go with you to the end —
  Take your burden to the Lord and leave it there.

It was in 1951 that I dared to sing this song as a duet
with another Elim pastor who is my closest friend, at
the church in Winton, Bournemouth, where I was the
pastor. Fortunately his voice was (and still is) very
good, as well as his performance at the piano. Afterwards one of my church members suggested we were
better gifted for the stage than for the pulpit! So, when
I found the story of how this hymn came to be written
I decided it had to have a place in this book.

It was composed in 1916 by a Methodist pastor who
was born into slavery in Berline, Maryland, USA, on
7th July 1851 and, to add to his grief, by the time he
was five years old he was an orphan. He was Charles
Tindley. But with the grit of other young Negroes he
decided he was not going to be put down. He taught
himself to read and write, enlisted in one of Philadelphia's night schools, then took a correspondence course
with the Boston School of Theology and graduated as an
expert linguist in both Hebrew and Greek. To support
himself he worked as caretaker of the Calvary Methodist Episcopal Church. After gaining his degrees with
distinction in theology he became a Methodist minister,
and — what says as much for the church as it does for
Charles — he returned to Calvary Methodist Church as
its minister when he was fifty-one years of age. In fact,
the church prospered under his ministry to the extent
that its membership increased to 12,500 thus necessitat-
ing a larger church building which was named after
him, Tindley Temple Methodist Church.

This was not the only popular hymn that he authored. Others include 'Nothing Between', 'By and By'
and 'Stand by me'. He also composed a song in 1901
which began, 'I'll Overcome Some Day'. Little did he
realize, at the time, that Dr Martin Luther King would
lead the civil rights marches singing an adaptation of
this song altering the words to 'We Shall Overcome'.
He was not only a gifted author, composer, academic

and considerate pastor but he also had a practical turn of mind. One day one of his church members came to him loaded down with trouble and looking for comfort from her pastor. 'Put all your troubles in a sack,' he told her, 'then take 'em to the Lord and leave them there.'

After the woman had left and as he sat in his study those words lingered in his mind. Then slowly as these thoughts circulated in his mind he took up his pen and began to write:

> Leave it there, leave it there, take your burden to the Lord and leave it there; if you trust and never doubt, He will surely bring you out — Take your burden to the Lord and leave it there.

And I especially like these his second and third verses when I think of those who suffer physically, and others who have been let down by their friends just at the time when they need a friend in deed. Loyalty commands a high place in my priorities, and that has been the mark of friendship with my friend.

I believe Charles Tindley had the psalmist's words in mind when he wrote his lines,

> When I remember these things, I pour out my soul in me: for I had gone with the multitude, I went with them to the house of God, with the voice of joy and praise, with a multitude that kept holyday. Why art thou cast down, O my soul? and why art thou disquieted in me? hope thou in God; for I shall yet praise him for the help of his countenance (Psalm 42: 4–5).

In my fanciful imagination I think of the psalmist, who had been thrust out of his rightful place in Israel, thrusting his hand under his shirt and, metaphorically, taking out his soul, and placing it in the palm of his hand then giving it a talking to: 'Take courage, my soul! Do you remember those times (but how could you ever forget them!) when you led a great procession to the Temple on festival days, singing with joy, praising the Lord? Why then be down cast? Why be discouraged and sad? Hope in God! I shall yet praise him again. Yes, I shall again praise him for his help' (TLB).

(Footnote: My Elim pastor friend from those Winton days did not go on the stage. In fact, he became the General Superintendent of the Elim Churches of Great Britain and a distinguished statesman in the churches of the World Pentecostal Movement. His name? The Revd Dr Eldin Corsie!)

Low in the grave he lay

1 Low in the grave he lay,
  Jesus, my Saviour;
  Waiting the coming day,
  Jesus, my Lord.
    Up from the grave he rose,
    With a mighty triumph o'er his foes;
    He arose a victor from the dark domain,
    And he lives for ever with his saints to reign:
    He arose! He arose! Hallelujah! Christ arose!

2 Vainly they watch his bed,
  Jesus, my Saviour;
  Vainly they seal the dead,
  Jesus, my Lord,
    Up from the grave . . .

3 Death cannot keep his prey,
  Jesus, my Saviour,
  He tore the bars away,
  Jesus, my Lord.
    Up from the grave . . .

I've known this hymn since my childhood but its strongest memory is the thrill I experienced leading the singing of it by a congregation of over six thousand in the Royal Albert Hall at the Elim Church's Easter Monday meetings. The 'rafters' in the hall's dome literally quivered with the vibrations from these thousands of Christians as they burst into the refrain:

Up from the grave he arose,
With a mighty triumph o'er his foes;
He arose a victor from the dark domain,

And he lives forever with his saints to reign:
He arose! He arose! Hallelujah! Christ arose!

When I read the challenge of Mordecai to Esther as she
hesitated to plead with her husband, King Ahasuerus,
on behalf of the Jews, 'Who knows if you have come
to the kingdom for such a time as this?', I dreamed of
where I would like to have been born in man's time
on earth. It must be for me the days following the
resurrection of Jesus when Christians in Jerusalem greeted each other with the words, 'Alleluia! He is arisen!'
and the response would be, 'Alleluia! He is risen
indeed!' Wouldn't it be nice if we greeted each other
like that each Easter Sunday?

Robert Lowry was attracted to this thought when
he wrote this hymn. During his private devotions one
evening in the Easter season of 1874 he was reading
Luke's account of the women who went to the sep-
ulchre to anoint the body of Jesus and encountered two
angels who said: 'Why seek ye the living among the
dead? He is not here, but is risen; remember how he
spake unto you when he was yet in Galilee, saying,
The Son of man must be delivered into the hands of
sinful men, and be crucified, and the third day rise
again.' Then there follows this simple, yet very impor-
tant comment, 'And they remembered his words!'

Robert Lowry was so inspired by the reading of this
story that he went to his little harmonium and began
to play as the words came into his mind, Low in the
grave he lay — Jesus, my Saviour! Waiting the coming
day, Jesus my Lord!

Robert, who was born in Philadelphia, USA, on 12th
March 1826, made a commitment to Christ when he was
seventeen. He studied at Bucknell University where he
was to become Professor of Literature. He subsequently
served as pastor of Baptist Churches in Philadelphia,
New Jersey, New York City and Brooklyn. He wrote

many favourite gospel hymns including, 'Shall we gather at the river' and 'What can wash away my stain?'

When he was asked how he came to write his hymns he said (and this may be helpful to would-be hymn-writers of today):

I have no set method. Sometimes the music comes and the words follow. I watch my moods, and when anything strikes me, whether words or music, no matter where I am, at home, on the street, I jot it down. My brain is in a sort of spinning machine, for there is music running through it all the time. The tunes of nearly all the hymns I have written have been completed on paper, before I tried them on the organ. Frequently, the words of the hymn and the music have been written at the same time.

May the mind

1 May the mind of Christ my Saviour
   Live in me from day to day,
   By his love and power controlling
   All I do and say.

2 May the word of God dwell richly
   In my heart from hour to hour,
   So that all may see I triumph
   Only through his power.

3 May the peace of God my Father
   Rule my life in everything,
   That I may be calm to comfort
   Sick and sorrowing.

4 May the love of Jesus fill me,
   As the waters fill the sea;
   Him exalting, self abasing,
   This is victory.

5 May I run the race before me,
   Strong and brave to face the foe,
   Looking only unto Jesus,
   As I onward go.

Katie Barclay Wilkinson wrote this hymn some time before 1913, but it was not published until 1925 by CSSM in its hymn-book Golden Bells.

Little is known of Mrs Wilkinson. She was born in 1859 and belonged to the Anglican Church and was an active member in West London amongst young women. She was living in Kensington, London, when she died on 28th December 1928, but her husband, Frederick

Barclay Wilkinson, outlived her by nine years having moved to Leytonstone, Essex, after his wife's death.

Though this hymn was designed for young people in the evangelical wing of the Church of England it has since become popular in a wider circle. It is a beautiful prayer, simple in style and comprehensive in its spiritual aspirations. In all probability Katie based it on Paul's letter to the Philippians (2:5) where he encourages his favourite church (cf chapter 1:3) to follow the mind of Christ which was epitomized in his humility and sacrificial service. In fact the verses of Philippians chapter 2 (5 to 11) were used as a hymn by the Early Church and they linked them with the frequently quoted prophecies of Isaiah in chapter 53.

Christ's mind in us means that his love will be present to control us, his Word to sustain us, his peace to calm us, and his example to guide us. Another interesting feature of the hymn is seen in the words of this verse: 'May I run the race before me, strong and brave to face the foe, looking only unto Jesus as I onward go.'

Here Mrs Wilkinson draws on the imagery of the figure of a runner in a race which we find in Hebrews 12:1: 'Let us run with patience the race that is set before us.' The secret of success for the runner is given in verses 2 and 3 of that chapter which is in these two phrases: 'looking unto Jesus the author and finisher of our faith' and 'consider him that endured such contradiction of sinners against himself, lest ye be wearied and faint in your minds.'

A good piece of psychology for the runner is found here. He is told to look to Jesus the alpha and omega of our faith, that is, the one who embodies the completeness of our faith. Everything for and about our Christian faith is right here in Jesus. So, as we keep looking to Jesus as we keep running, the active part of our Christian life, we will be kept true and heading for the right winning-post.

The next phrase, 'consider him', refers to the contemplative side of the Christian life. This is where we are encouraged to employ Christian meditation, which provides the incentive — hence strength — for the active side of Christianity. And for this you have to stop and *consider* the life of Christ in all its beauty and perfection. I love travelling through Switzerland by road and rail, but to enjoy the beauty of the alpine flowers I must leave the train and the car and walk slowly in the mountains and then stop and soak in the beauty of nature.

So Mrs Wilkinson embraced a great deal of sound Christian sense in this hymn for young people.

Katie also wrote a sixth verse, and I think it is a pity that it has been omitted from many of our hymn-books:

> May his beauty rest upon us
> As I seek the lost to win,
> And may they forget the channel,
> Seeing only him.

There are two tunes married to these words. 'St Leonard's (Gould)' was composed by the Revd Arthur Cyril Barham-Gould when he was living at St Leonard's-on-Sea, East Sussex. He was curate in two of London's evangelical parishes, All Souls, Langham Place, and Holy Trinity, Brompton, and then Vicar of St Paul's, Onslow Square, London from 1936 until his death in 1953.

John Wilson, the grand octagenarian gentleman of British church music now living in Guildford, composed the tune 'Griffin's Brook', especially for Mrs Wilkinson's hymn. He was born into the Cadbury family (on his mother's side, Margaret Davies) in the nineteenth-century garden village of Bournville, near Birmingham, on 21st January 1905. He graduated in physics and mathematics at Cambridge, but at age twenty-three entered the Royal College of Music maybe through the influence of his uncle, Sir Walford Davies, with whom he lodged. Most of his working life has been at Charterhouse where he was Director of Music, and as a teacher at the Royal College of Music. He named the tune after the brook that runs through the garden village of Bournville.

Mine eyes have seen the glory of the coming of the Lord

1 Mine eyes have seen the glory of the coming of the
   Lord.
   He is trampling out the vintage where the grapes
   of wrath are stored;
   He hath loosed the fatal lightning of his terrible
   swift sword:
   His truth is marching on.
   Glory, glory, Alleluia!
   Glory, glory, Alleluia!
   Glory, glory, Alleluia!
   His truth is marching on.

2 He hath sounded forth the trumpet that shall never
   call retreat;
   He is sifting out the hearts of men before his
   judgement-seat;
   O, be swift, my soul, to answer him; be jubilant,
   my feet!
   Our God is marching on.
   Glory, glory, alleluia!
   Glory, glory, alleluia!
   Glory, glory, alleluia!
   Our God is marching on.

3 In the beauty of the lilies Christ was born across the
   sea,
   With a glory in his bosom that transfigures you and
   me:
   As he died to make men holy, let us live to make
   men free,
   While God is marching on.
   Glory, glory, alleluia!
   Glory, glory, alleluia!

   Glory, glory, alleluia!
   While God is marching on.

4 He is coming like the glory of the morning on the
   wave;
  He is wisdom to the mighty; he is succour to the
   brave;
  So the world shall be his footstool, and the soul of
   time his slave:
  Our God is marching on.
   Glory, glory, alleluia!
   Glory, glory, alleluia!
   Glory, glory, alleluia!
   Our God is marching on.

This hymn was projected into public attention by it
being chosen as one of the hymns for the memorial
service of Sir Winston Churchill, although it is rarely
used in British church services.

The words were written by Mrs Julia Howe and first
printed in the *New York Daily Tribune* on 14th January
1862, it is thought without her authority. A month later
Mrs Howe submitted her poem to the editor of the
Atlantic Monthly who paid her five dollars, publishing
it with the title 'The Battle Hymn of the Republic'.

The story of the hymn's evolution begins with the
tune which seems to have started its life with a musician
from Philadelphia who was commissioned to write a
song for a fire company in South Carolina in the 1850s
which began with the line, 'Say, bummers, will you
meet us'. It then had a varied life, being used by the
Methodist Sunday Schools with different words, 'Say,
brother, will you meet us', even crossing the Atlantic to
the United Kingdom where the organist of the Temple
Church, E. J. Hopkins, arranged it in four parts. It was
then adopted by a quartet of sergeants, one of whom

was a friendly Scot called John Brown.

There was another John Brown of those days, who was an ardent campaigner against slavery, and in those pre-enlightened days was to be hanged for his worthy crusade. So, Sergeant Brown's fellow soldiers, in what some thought to be of poor taste, made a joke of it, singing as they marched along that though the abolitionist John Brown was dead his soul was still marching on in the soldier Sergeant John Brown.

It became a popular marching song heard by Julia Howe and her husband in the company of a friend, the Revd James Clark, when they attended the review by President Lincoln of the Union Troops at Bailey's Cross Roads, Virginia on 20th November 1861. As they heard the soldiers sing, Mr Clark whispered in Mrs Howe's ear that maybe she could write some better words for the catchy tune. That night in the light of a candle while her husband slept she wrote the words of this hymn.

There are two widely differing accounts of where she wrote her lines. The first says that it was in the comfort of the Willard Hotel, Washington, that inspiration came to her. The second gives the more romantic story that it was as Mrs Howe lay on an uncomfortable camp bed in a canvas tent, similar to the ones used by Lincoln's troops, that she wrote the hymn. But both accounts agree that it was written on the headed paper of the Sanitary Commission in Washington to which her husband belonged.

Julia Ward Howe was born in New York on 27th May 1819. This was her married name, her husband being a banker and philanthropist according to story one, or a medical doctor according to story two! I wonder if he could have been both? We do know that both husband and wife were writers and Julia a poetess. They were also staunch workers for the advancement of women and the abolition of slavery, so it is appropriate that she should have written this hymn with its association with the abolitionist Brown. Julia's husband was highly regarded and the hymn-writer John Greefleaf Whittier thought so too and commends him highly in a poem he wrote in his honour called, *The Hero*. Mrs Howe died in Middletown, Rhode Island, on 17th October 1910.

1 Morning has broken, like the first morning;
  Blackbird has spoken like the first bird.
  Praise for the singing!
  Praise for the morning!
  Praise for them, springing fresh from the Word!

2 Sweet the rain's new fall sunlit from heaven,
  Like the first dewfall on the first grass.
  Praise for the sweetness of the wet garden,
  Sprung in completeness where his feet pass.

3 Mine is the sunlight! Mine is the morning
  Born of the one light Eden saw play!
  Praise with elation, praise every morning,
  God's re-creation of the new day!

This hymn has to be included in my collection if only because the tune 'Bunessan', to which it is set, is played as a signature tune every Sunday morning at 6.30 on BBC Radio 4. Strangely it has attracted more criticism from listeners than anything else on the programme, not because of the tune but of the arrangement. I am ambivalent about it because the percentage who complain is small, and in broadcasting you soon learn that it is impossible to please all your listeners!

Other people involved in its composition and success also sit somewhat uncomfortably in the company of other hymn-writers in this book. To begin with, Cat Stevens, who as a singer of popular songs in the seventies took his recording of it into the first ten in *Top of the Pops* is a very active Muslim.

The author was Eleanor Farjeon, daughter of a playwright, novelist and journalist of Jewish descent. She had a peripatetic spiritual journey; having started out as an Anglican she had a brief encounter with spiritism, then a detour into a few theories of reincarnation, and towards the end of a Bohemian life style, when she was seventy, was received into the Roman Catholic Church. Her life was one long search for a deeper spiritual experience in life, and ultimately the writings of St Augustine and St Ignatius Loyola played an influential part in her turning towards Rome. The late Canon Percy Dearmer, to whom we owe a debt of gratitude for his invaluable contribution to British hymnody, especially for the *English Hymnal*, was a friend of Eleanor. He was also editor of the hymn-book *Songs of Praise*, which he published in 1925.

Its immediate success suggested the necessity for a further new edition which allowed him to make some revisions and additions. This gave him the opportunity to invite Eleanor Farjeon to compose a hymn which would be happy and bright for the beginning of a new day and which could be set to the Gaelic tune 'Bunessan'. She took for her opening theme the words in Genesis 1:5 'And God called the light, day', and gave it the title, 'Thanks for the day'. But when it was republished as a poem in 1957 she changed it to, 'A morning song, for the first day of Spring'.

Eleanor Farjeon was born in the heart of the British Empire, as it then was, in Westminster, London, on 13th February 1881, into a literary family and inherited her father's writing abilities. Among her works were *Nursery Rhymes of London, Faithful Jenny Dove, Singing Games from Arcady* and *The Children's Bells*. She also collaborated with her brother Herbert to write a rhyming history of England for children which was published in 1932 with the title *Kings and Queens*. She also wrote two plays, *The Two Bouquets* in 1936 and *The Glass Slipper* in 1944, which was made into a musical produced by Robert Donat.

One of the soloists was the up-and-coming singer Ian Wallace, whom we now hear regularly on the BBC's programme *My Music*. Prior to using the hymn for one of my broadcasts I asked for his recollections of Eleanor. He told me that she used to regularly visit St James' Theatre during rehearsals when he was part of the cast. She was a charming lady with a very serene face and round apple cheeks and a petite nose supporting thick pebble glasses. She was very short-sighted. But what amused him most was the day she arrived for the premier performance at this smart London theatre. The celebrities were there in their evening attire, but Eleanor, quite unabashed, mingled with the guests in the foyer wearing a long brown Harris-Tweed coat, an enormous woollen muffler, and long brown boots.

Though the radio programme *Morning Has Broken* is transmitted too early for some people, it follows an ancient tradition. In the year AD 110 Pliny, the Roman Governor of Bithynia, in one of his reports to the Emperor Trajan in Rome about the Christians of the Early Church said:

> They were in the habit of meeting on a certain fixed day before sunrise (on the southern shores of the Black Sea) and reciting an antiphonal hymn to Christ as God, and then binding themselves with an oath — not to commit any crime, but to abstain from all acts of theft, robbery and adultery, from breaches of faith, from denying a trust when called upon to honour it.

Bunessan is a place on the Isle of Mull which was the birthplace of the Scottish poet Mary Macdonald who used the melody in 1917 for some verses she wrote entitled 'Child in the manger'. The story is told that it was being sung by an itinerant Highland singer one day in the 1880s in his wanderings in Scotland when someone noted it for posterity.

I think these words in Job (38:7) would be an appropriate appendage to this beautiful hymn of praise:

When the morning stars sang together,
and all the sons of God shouted for joy?

My hope is built on nothing less

1 My hope is built on nothing less
  Than Jesus' blood and righteousness;
  I dare not trust my sweetest frame,
  But wholly lean on Jesus' Name.
    On Christ, the solid rock, I stand;
    All other ground is sinking sand.

2 When darkness seems to veil his face,
  I rest on his unchanging grace;
  In every high and stormy gale,
  My anchor holds within the veil:

3 His oath, his covenant, and blood,
  Support me in the whelming flood;
  When all around my soul gives way,
  He then is all my hope and stay:

Edward Mote, the author of this popular evangelical
hymn, was born on 21st January 1797 into a poor home
where the name of Christ was only a swear-word. His
parents were publicans and with no interest in Christianity with the result that his Sundays were spent roam-
ing London's streets. He said, 'So ignorant was I that I
did not know that there was a God.' Even the school
he attended forbade any teaching from the Bible. However, when he left school he found work as an apprentice to a cabinet-maker who was a Christian. So it was
that at the age of sixteen he accompanied his boss to a
meeting at Tottenham Court Chapel. The remarkable —
but are there ever coincidences in the ways of God —
development in the life of Edward Mote was that this
led to him finding Christ.

He continued in his trade with much success and then he discovered that he also possessed the gift of preaching, and it was through his visit to a meeting in Lisle Street, near Piccadilly Circus in London's West End, that he was encouraged to publish this hymn. This was in 1834. Here is his own account of how he came to write this hymn, and I believe it was the first of over a hundred hymns which he wrote:

One morning it came into my mind as I went to labour, to write an hymn on the 'Gracious Experience of a Christian'. As I went up Holborn (London) I had the chorus, 'On Christ the solid rock I stand, all other ground is sinking sand'. In the day, I had the first four verses complete, and wrote them off. On the Sabbath following, I met Brother King as I came out of the Lisle Street Meeting . . . who informed me that his wife was very ill, and asked me to call and see her. I had an early tea and called afterwards. He said that it was his usual custom to sing a hymn, read a portion, and engage in prayer, before he went to the meeting. He looked for his hymn-book, but could find it nowhere. I said, 'I have some verses in my pocket; if you like, we could sing them.' We did, and his wife enjoyed them so much that after the service he asked me, as a favour, to leave a copy of them for his wife. I went home, and by the fireside composed the last two verses, wrote them off, and took them to Sister King. As these verses so met the dying woman's case, my attention to them was the more arrested, and I had a thousand of them printed for distribution. I sent one to the *Spiritual Magazine*, without my initials, which appeared some time after this. Brother Rees, of Crown Street, Soho, brought out an edition of hymns in 1836, and this hymn was in it. David Denham introduced it in 1837 with Rees' name given as the author.

Many popular hymns are of the testimony-type which are frequently criticized. This is a clear statement of faith, and brings to mind Paul's words in 1 Corinthians 3:11' 'For other foundation can no man lay than that is laid, which is Jesus Christ.'

In 1848 he was called to the pastorate of a Baptist congregation in Horsham, West Sussex, and four years later when Edward Mote was fifty-five he was largely instrumental in erecting a building for his congregation. The church officers and members were so appreciative that they offered him the deeds to the property. He declined the offer saying: 'I do not want the chapel; I only want the pulpit, and when I cease to preach Christ, then turn me out of that.' However, he ministered at the church for the rest of his life. He once said, 'The truths I have been preaching, I am now living upon, and they do very well to die upon.' He died at the age of seventy-seven and is buried in the churchyard.

Now thank we all our God

1 Now thank we all our God,
   With hearts, and hands, and voices;
   Who wondrous things hath done,
   In whom his world rejoices;
   Who, from our mother's arms,
   Hath blessed us on our way
   With countless gifts of love,
   And still is ours today.

2 O may this bounteous God
   Through all our life be near us,
   With ever-joyful hearts
   And blessed peace to cheer us;
   And keep us in his grace,
   And guide us when perplexed,
   And free us from all ills
   In this world and the next.

3 All praise and thanks to God
   The Father now be given,
   The Son, and him who reigns
   With them in highest heaven;
   The one eternal God,
   Whom heaven and earth adore;
   For thus it was, is now,
   And shall be evermore.

I am repeatedly astonished (I don't think that is too strong a word) by the incredible fortitude and faith of many of our hymn-writers. This is an example.

The author was Martin Rinkart who was born in Eilenberg on 23rd April 1586. He was the only pastor of the walled town of Eilenberg in Saxony for nineteen of the Thirty Years' War. This was the name given to a series of wars in Germany in the seventeenth century which, like so many wars, began for religious reasons. It was particularly vicious with horrendous loss of life. Rinkart's walled town was a haven for refugees bringing with them the effects of the plague and over-taxing the town's resources so that famine and disease were rampant. In the great plague of 1637 Martin Rinkart read the burial service for five thousand of the inhabitants, one of whom was his wife!

This frail and faithful pastor continued to minister to his people though he himself faced bloodthirsty lawless bands of roving soldiers. It is in this situation that I find it so astonishing that he should find the reserve to write this hymn of worship and praise, of which, incidentally, the first two verses were written as a grace for mealtimes for his children. He based them on Ecclesiasticus 50:22–24:

Now therefore bless ye the Lord of all, which only doeth wondrous things everywhere, which exalteth our days from the womb, and dealeth with us according to his mercy. He grant us joyfulness of heart, and that peace may be in our days in Israel forever. That he would confirm his mercy with us, and deliver us at his time.

He later added the third verse which is a paraphrase of the Gloria and thought to have been published in 1636. However, the earliest surviving text is with the tune *Nun Danket* in composer Johann Crüger's *Praxis Pietatis Melica* of 1647. Johann Sebastian Bach used the words and tune for his Cantata 192 which has been called the 'German Te Deum'.

Martin Rinkart who was a skilled musician, was crowned a poet when he was thirty-eight years old (three years before he was appointed pastor in Eilenberg), wrote a cycle of seven dramas to depict events in the Reformation, and authored many hymns.

We are indebted to Catherine Winkworth for the English translation. According to Julian, Catherine was born in London on 13th September 1829. She published the hymn as we have it in our hymn-books in her *Lyra Germanica* (Second Series) in 1858 under the delightful heading 'The Chorus of God's Thankful Children'. Her early life was spent in Manchester, before she moved to Clifton, Bristol. It was there she took a keen interest in the higher education of women and assisted in the founding of the University of Bristol. Canon Frank Colquhoun credits her with the title 'Queen of Translators', and her output was quite formidable, 400 hymns from German into English. Dr Percival of Clifton College wrote (in 1878); 'She was a person of remarkable intellectual and social gifts, and very unusual attainments . . . with a certain tender and sympathetic refinement.' 'Now thank we all our God' is usually sung to the tune *Nun Danket*, composed by Johann Crüger, which first appeared in printed form in 1647 with its German text.

O for a closer walk with God

1 O for a closer walk with God,
  A calm and heavenly frame,
  A light to shine upon the road
  That leads me to the Lamb.

2 Where is the blessedness I knew
  When first I saw the Lord?
  Where is that soul-refreshing view
  Of Jesus and his word?

3 What peaceful hours I once enjoyed!
  How sweet the memory still!
  But they have left an aching void
  The world can never fill.

4 Return, Oh holy Dove! return,
  Sweet messenger of rest!
  I hate the sins that made thee mourn,
  And drove thee from my breast.

5 The dearest idol I have known,
  Whate'er that idol be,
  Help me to tear it from thy throne,
  And worship only thee.

6 So shall my walk be close to God,
  Calm and serene my frame;
  So purer light shall mark the road
  That leads me to the Lamb.

One of the unanswerable questions I was soon to be asked as a young pastor is encapsulated in this one word by someone in pain, 'Why?' And now, fifty years on, I cannot always give a satisfactory answer. However, there are times when one has glimpses of the sun even though dark clouds hang low. This is the story of this hymn.

William Cowper, the author, was plagued by mental suffering from his earliest days. He was the fourth child of the Revd John and Anne Cowper, but soon William was to find himself the only child through the death of his two brothers and sister in infancy. Even so his early days with his mother were happy although short-lived, because just prior to his sixth birthday she died when giving birth to his brother John. Days of suffering followed at his boarding school where William, a gentle and sensitive lad, was subjected to severe bullying.

In his teens he fell madly in love with his cousin Theodara but her father blocked the marriage, and both Theodara and William were to remain unmarried for the rest of their lives. This rejection inevitably took its toll on William. Following his call to the Bar, and though enjoying many successful *experiments* with his poetry and prose, he suffered a severe breakdown which resulted in several attempts at suicide. He was subsequently obliged to seek treatment at the Collegion Insanorium in St Albans, a private mental hospital, and it was here that a shaft of sunlight broke through the clouds of depression when his only surviving brother John visited him and spoke to him of God's love and forgiveness. This made a deep impression on him and can be seen reflected in verses 2 and 3 of this hymn, which he was to write some years later.

It was around this time that he met the Revd Morley Unwin and his wife Mary, who opened their home to him. He took up gardening and in a letter to one of his relatives in March 1767 he said: 'I am become a great Florist and Shrub-doctor.' And this part of his life was to inspire him to give us the hymn, 'Hark, my soul! it is the Lord . . . Sought thee wandering, set thee right;

turned the darkness into light.' But pain was to strike
again when his friend the Revd Morley Unwin was
killed in a riding accident. However, the silver lining to
this cloud came in the form of the ex-slave ship captain
John Newton entering his life. As the local parson he
called to offer condolences to Mrs Unwin. The friendship that developed between Newton and William
Cowper, along with Mary Unwin and her daughter,
resulted in them taking up residence in Orchard Side,
Market Square, Olney. This is now a museum and still
open to visitors.

The birth of this moving hymn occurred during
another period of melancholy, and it once again shows
how God uses some of our most painful experiences to
inspire the greatest thoughts. The verses of 'O for a
closer walk with God' were composed through the long
winter hours of a very dark night when William was in
despair. We know it was written on 9th December 1769
because he referred to it in a letter to a friend the
following day. He wrote: 'I began to compose them
yesterday morning, but fell asleep at the end of the first
two lines. When I awakened again the third and fourth
were whispered to my heart, in a way which I have
often experienced.' The hymn was headed 'Walking
with God' and is based on Genesis chapter 5, verse 24:
'Enoch walked with God, and he was not for God took
him.'

The other feature of the hymn worth mentioning was
that Cowper's despair was on account of the illness of
Mrs Unwin when he thought she was going to die. He
had come to depend on her to such an extent that he
felt he could not live without her. But during these dark
hours of this night God spoke to him and he saw that
his love for Mary had come between him and God and
was destroying the blessedness he knew when first he
saw the Lord (this is the reference to his brother's visit
to the mental hospital and his commitment to Christ).

The result was that he decided to ask God for strength to correct this position. 'The dearest idol I have known, whate'er that idol be, help me to tear it from thy throne, and worship only thee. So shall my walk be close with God, calm and serene my frame.'

Newton moved to London in 1780 and six years later Cowper and Mrs Unwin went to live in Weston Underwood followed by his final change of residence in 1796 to East Dereham. It was there his great friend Mary died, which sadly left him again in despair. Four years later he also went to his eternal rest on 25th April 1800.

O Love that wilt not let me go

1 O Love that wilt not let me go,
   I rest my weary soul in thee;
   I give thee back the life I owe,
   That in thine ocean depths its flow
   May richer, fuller be.

2 O Light that followest all my way,
   I yield my flickering torch to thee;
   My heart restores its borrowed ray,
   That in thy sunshine's blaze its day
   May brighter, fairer be.

3 O Joy that seekest me through pain,
   I cannot close my heart to thee;
   I trace the rainbow through the rain,
   And feel the promise is not vain
   That morn shall tearless be.

4 O Cross that liftest up my head,
   I dare not ask to fly from thee;
   I lay in dust life's glory dead,
   And from the ground there blossoms red
   Life that shall endless be.

When I was a young minister in Bournemouth I attempted to preach on the problem of pain. Now that I am much older, and, I hope, wiser, I would approach the subject far differently. C. S. Lewis when discussing the subject in his book of that title, suggested that 'God shouts to us in our pain.'

I believe that the intimate relationship with God that enabled George Matheson to write this hymn was refined by the painful circumstances of his life, not least his blindness since the age of eighteen. He was born in Glasgow on 27th March 1842 and though he never enjoyed full sight he continued with his education and eventually entered the University of Glasgow. He proved to be a brilliant scholar, and then went on to read theology in preparation for his ordination in the Church.

He was forty-four years of age when he was inducted as pastor of the 2000 strong St Bernard's Parish Church, Edinburgh. Though he was never to marry he enjoyed the faithful companionship and academic help of his sister who studied and became proficient in Greek, Latin and Hebrew for the sole purpose of becoming the 'eyes' of her much-loved brother.

There are different stories of how this very moving hymn came to be written, such as the one of the unrequited love of a Scottish maiden, but this has never been satisfactorily substantiated until Ian Bradley's book, *The Penguin Book of Hymns*.

He also suffered pain and anguish of mind in his attempts to come to terms with his own doubts. 'At one time, with a great thrill of horror,' he once told a friend, 'I found myself an absolute atheist. After being ordained at Innellan, I believed nothing, neither God nor immortality. I tendered my resignation to the Presbytery, but to their honour they would not accept it, even a Highland Presbytery. They said I was a young man and would change. I have changed!' And so it is no wonder that he wrote:

> O Love that wilt not let me go,
> I rest my weary soul in thee;
> I give thee back the life I owe,
> That in thine ocean depths its flow
> May richer, fuller be.

Before George Matheson died on 28th August 1906 at

Avenelle House, North Berwick, East Lothian, he left
his own version of how he came to write his hymn:

> My hymn was composed in the manse of Innellan
> on the evening of 6th of June 1882. I was at that time
> alone. It was the day of my sister's marriage, and the
> rest of the family were staying overnight in Glasgow.
> Something had happened to me, which was known
> only to myself, and which caused me the most severe
> mental suffering. The hymn was the fruit of that
> suffering. It was the quickest bit of work I ever did
> in my life. I had the impression rather of having it
> dictated to me by some inward voice than of working
> it out myself. I am quite sure that the whole work
> was completed in five minutes, and equally sure it
> never received at my hands any retouching or correc-
> tion. I have no natural gift of rhythm. All the other
> verses I have ever written are manufactured articles;
> this came like a day spring from on high. I have
> never been able to gain once more the same fervour
> in verse.

Matheson's hymn was first published in the well-
known magazine *Life and Work* in January 1883 and a
year later the celebrated Scottish church organist, Dr
Albert Peace, was asked by the Scottish Hymnal Committee to compose the tune. In a letter to a friend he
gave this account of how he wrote it:

> It was composed in 1884 during the time of the music
> of the *Scottish Hymnal*, of which I was the musical
> editor, was in preparation. I wrote it at Brodick
> Manse, where I was on a visit to my old friend Mr
> M'Lean. There was no tune of that particular metre
> available at that time, so I was requested by Hymnal
> Committee to write one specially for Dr Matheson's
> hymn. After reading it over carefully, I wrote the

music straight off, and may say that the ink of the first note was hardly dry when I had finished the tune.

Albert Lister Peace was born in Huddersfield in 1844, and he was only nine years old when he became organist at Holmfrith parish church.

Oh, the love of my Lord

1 Oh, the love of my Lord is the essence
  Of all that I love here on earth.
  All the beauty I see
  He has given to me
  And his giving is gentle as silence.

2 Every day, every hour, every moment
  Have been blessed by the strength of his love.
  At the turn of each tide
  He is there at my side,
  And his touch is as gentle as silence.

3 There've been times when I've turned from his
    presence
  And I've walked other paths, other ways.
  But I've called on his name
  In the dark of my shame,
  And his mercy was gentle as silence.

This is one of the hymns that has produced a great deal
of listener response to the BBC Radio 4's programme
Morning Has Broken during the time I have been present-
ing. It is from one of today's hymn-writers, a very
humble lady who was destined to be a nun but was
obliged to return to the schoolroom as a teacher. The
author is Estelle White, who has composed the tune
which has equal simplicity and is ideally suited to her
words. I well remember the occasion when my producer, Claire Campbell-Smith, played it to me in the
studio at Broadcasting House. It was a recording by the
choir of Waltham Abbey and as I sat with my cans
(headphones) fastened to my ears several pictures
appeared in my mind.

First, there was the Virgin Mary as she watched Jesus grow. She knew that a sword was to pierce her soul before the end of his earthly pilgrimage, but here she is seen to derive strength from his presence as she cared for his earthly needs.

Next we have another Mary, the sister of Lazarus. She was able to see the greater value there was in what she could do for this Jesus in just *being* with him rather than *doing* for him.

Finally, there has to be — may I say, of course — the unnamed woman of the streets who was despised by Simon the Pharisee as she prostrated herself in his elegant home on the main boulevard of Jerusalem, washing the feet of Jesus with her tears. But that was not all! She had saved for her own self some very expensive perfume. She had kept this exquisite aroma to sweeten the time of her death, and it had long been hidden in the safe confidentiality of an unseen corner of her humble home. But now was her opportunity to open the door of love in her heart as she poured over his feet this costly perfume.

Of her Jesus said, 'Her sins, and they are many, are forgiven, for she loved much (Luke 7:47).

Estelle has lived a varied and interesting life. She was born in Tyneside on 4th December 1925, and in 1943 after grammar school she decided to make her contribution to the country's war service by joining the ATS as a Bandswoman and a member of the Headquarters Staff Military Band. After her demobilization she qualified as a Chartered Physiotherapist, working in hospitals in the United Kingdom and Canada. It was then in 1964 that she heard the call to enter a Religious Order. Though she would have wished it to be otherwise she was obliged to leave the Order in 1970 without taking her final vows, and devoted the rest of her life to teaching RE and Music in our schools.

She has authored over a hundred short works of

worship including hymns, Mass settings and psalm settings and, it seems somewhat incongruously, is a keen
supporter of Yorkshire County Cricket Club. I have a
picture of her on the boundary waving the YCC flag as
Boycott scores yet another of his many centuries. It's
no wonder her hymns have the human touch!

Estelle (in her retirement!) has qualified as an MA at
Leeds University, and is now taking her Ph.D. in 'The
Biblical Traditions of Irenaeus of Lyon'. When I inter-
viewed her for this book she told me that she thought
so little of this hymn that she decided not to submit it
to Kevin Mayhew, her publisher, with the other eleven.
Kevin shrewdly knew a good thing when it was before
him and, when this hymn arrived on his desk after
he had asked for one more hymn for his collection,
recognized its potential and told Estelle he thought it
one of her best.

O perfect Love

1 O perfect Love, all human thought transcending,
   Lowly we kneel in prayer before your throne,
   That theirs may be the love which knows no ending,
   Whom you for evermore now join as one.

2 O perfect Life, be now their full assurance
   Of tender charity, and steadfast faith,
   Of patient hope, and quiet brave endurance,
   With childlike trust that fears not pain or death.

3 Grant them the joy which brightens earthly sorrow;
   Grant them the peace which calms all earthly strife;
   And to life's day the glorious unknown morrow
   That dawns upon eternal love and life.

'What's the use of a sister who composes poetry if she cannot write me new words to this tune?' That was the petulant question from a twenty-two year-old bride-to-be, Katherine Blomfield, directed to her twenty-five year-old sister, Dorothy, one Sunday evening in the early months of 1883 when the Blomfield family were spending a winter holiday at Howsley Cottage, Brathay, near Ambleside, in the Lake District. The tune the bride-to-be and her fiancé found just right for their wedding was by John Bacchus Dykes for the hymn 'Strength and Stay' but as the words contained the phrase 'the brightness of a holy death-bed' they needed new words.

Without any complaint Dorothy quietly left the room saying, 'Well, if no one will disturb me I will go into the library and see what I can do.' Fifteen minutes later she returned to the family and held out a sheet of paper to her younger sister containing the words of this hymn beginning, 'O perfect love, all human thought transcending, lowly we kneel in prayer before thy throne . . .'

Immediately their clergyman father called the mother and her four daughters with the one brother to the harmonium and they all joined in singing Dorothy's words to the tune of J. B. Dykes.

The family had returned to their holiday cottage after evening service and the main topic of conversation was Katherine's up-coming wedding to Dr Hugh Redmayne and the search was on for suitable hymns for her marriage service. The author made this note of the occasion in her diary:

> It went perfectly, and my sister was delighted, saying that it must be sung at her wedding. The writing of it was no effort after the initial idea had come to me of the two-fold aspect of perfect union of love and life, and I have always felt that God helped me to write it.

At first the hymn was only used at the weddings of friends and acquaintances but in 1889 it was included in the supplement to *Hymns Ancient and Modern* and then brought to the attention of Queen Victoria's granddaughter, Princess Louise, who chose it for her wedding to the Duke of Fife in July of that year. However, the Princess was not attracted to the tune of Dykes which had brought about Dorothy Gurney's words, so the Princess asked Sir Joseph Barnby to compose a different musical setting. He agreed and adapted one of his melodies to fit the verses and named it 'Sandringham' after the Royal residence in Norfolk.

The hymn's author was born Dorothy Frances Blomfield in 1858, the first of five children for the Revd and Mrs Frederick Blomfield. It was just one year after her paternal grandfather, the Rt Revd C. J. Blomfield, former Bishop of London, had died. She was to grow into adulthood seeing her three sisters and brother marry, before she met Gerald Gurney an Anglican priest whom she married when she was forty years of age. Just over twenty years later they were both received into the Roman Catholic Church. She was a resident of Notting Hill in the London borough of Kensington when she died on 15th June 1932.

This is the only hymn by which she is remembered, but her poem *God's Garden* was also very popular, especially the verse,

> The kiss of the sun for pardon,
> The song of the birds for mirth,
> One is nearer God's heart in a garden,
> Than anywhere else on earth.

O soul, are you weary and troubled? (Turn your eyes upon Jesus)

1 Oh soul, are you weary and troubled?
No light in the darkness you see?
There's light for a look at the Saviour,
And life more abundant and free!
Turn your eyes upon Jesus,
Look full in his wonderful face;
And the things of earth will grow strangely dim
In the light of his glory and grace.

2 Through death into life everlasting
He passed and we follow him there;
Over us sin no more hath dominion,
For more than conquerors we are!
Turn your eyes . . .

3 His words shall not fail you he promised;
Believe him, and all will be well:
Then go to a world that is dying,
His perfect salvation to tell.
Turn your eyes . . .

As a hymn this is not very well known but I felt I had to include it for one reason: the ability of a song to reach the places where preaching fails to reach. It was written by Helen Lemmel in 1918, towards the end of the First World War.

In support let me tell you of a lady in my home church in Swansea. Her name was Mary Evans, a brilliant pianist who has long since gone for her heavenly reward. She would always be seated at the piano ahead of the Sunday morning service using her considerable musical skills to prepare the right spiritual atmosphere for the worship service. One Sunday morning a recently 'demobbed' ex-serviceman of the Second World War was passing the open doors of the church. Having witnessed some of the horrific scenes that inevitably confront men and women engaged in such a conflict, he felt utterly depressed about the future. However, hearing the delightful sound as Mary played the tune of this hymn, he stopped, entered the porch of the church and out of curiosity took a seat in one of the pews at the rear of the church. At the close of the service he sought out the minister, Leslie Green, who gently dealt with his many questions. When he eventually left it was as a newly-committed Christian. Mary told the young man that the words of the tune she had been playing was, 'Turn your eyes upon Jesus'.

I can think of no better recommendation to give to any one whether or not that one is a Christian. In fact, it is the ideal exhortation to give to the members of a congregation before it begins its act of worship, and to take their minds off such mundane things as treating the entry of ladies with new hats on Easter Day as a fashion parade.

Not only is this song an aid to worship but it is also an effective remedy for those who 'are weary and troubled'. And if anyone should think this too subjective an approach then I would remind them that it is based on the words of comfort uttered by our Lord: 'Come to me, all you who are weary and burdened and I will give you rest' (Matthew 11:28 NIV).

Helen Lemmel was born on 14th November 1864 in a place called Wardle, England (there are two places with this name — one near Nantwich, Cheshire and the other in Greater Manchester), the daughter of a Wesleyan Methodist minister. When Helen was twelve her family emigrated to the USA. After studying music and singing in Germany she used her great gifts in church concerts in the early part of this century. In later life she taught music and singing at the Moody Bible Institute in Chicago, and authored more than 500 hymns and poems. She lived to the grand old age of ninety-seven.

She wrote the words and composed the music for this gospel song one day in 1918 as a result of receiving a religious leaflet which included the words, 'So then, turn your eyes upon him, look full into his face and you will find that the things of earth will acquire a strange new dimness'. It was aptly called, 'Focused'. She could not free these words from her mind until 'suddenly', as she later wrote, 'it was as if I were commanded to stop and listen. I stood still, and singing in my soul and spirit was the chorus, with not one conscious moment of putting word to word to make rhyme, or note to note to make melody. The verses were written the same week, after the usual manner of composition, but none the less dictated by the Holy Spirit.'

Later that year it was published in pamphlet form in London and was featured at the north of England Bible Convention at Keswick and soon became popular with British congregations. Six years later it was published in the United States.

O worship the King

1 O worship the King,
   All-glorious above;
   O gratefully sing
   His power and his love;
   Our shield and defender,
   The ancient of days,
   Pavilioned in splendour,
   And girded with praise.

2 O tell of his might,
   O sing of his grace,
   Whose robe is the light,
   Whose canopy, space;
   His chariots of wrath
   The deep thunder-clouds form,
   And dark is his path
   On the wings of the storm.

3 The earth, with its store
   Of wonders untold,
   Almighty, thy power
   Hath founded of old:
   Hath stablished it fast
   By a changeless decree,
   And round it hath cast,
   Like a mantle, the sea.

4 Thy bountiful care
   What tongue can recite?
   ·It breathes in the air,
   It shines in the light,
   It streams from the hills,
   It descends to the plain,

And sweetly distils
In the dew and the rain.

5 Frail children of dust,
And feeble as frail,
In thee do we trust,
Nor find thee to fail:
They mercies, how tender,
How firm to the end,
Our Maker, defender,
Redeemer, and friend!

6 O Lord of all might,
How boundless thy love!
While angels delight
To hymn thee above,
The humbler creation,
Though feeble their lays,
With true adoration
Shall sing to thy praise.

I wonder what early memories come back to you with
the singing of this hymn? For me the earliest are the
morning assemblies of my school days in Cadle on the
outskirts of Swansea. But at the time I was completely
unaware of the richness of its history. Perhaps head-
masters who read this book should take note, and give
a short comment about the writing of the hymns they
use in their schools. From our experience at the BBC it
promises to be a popular feature.

The author of this hymn was a very distinguished
man, Sir Robert Grant. He was born in Bengal, India,
in 1779 where his father was a director of the East
India Company and an Indian philanthropist. He was
educated in Magdalene College, Cambridge, where he
later became a Fellow. His distinguished career in law

was crowned with his appointment as King's Serjeant
in the Court of the Duchy of Lancaster. He then entered
the House of Commons as a Member for Elgin, Inver-
ness, and then for Norwich and Finsbury. Later he
became a Privy Councilor and Judge Advocate-General,
and during 1833 he carried through a bill for the emancipation of the Jews. But a year later he returned to India,
the land he loved, as Governor of Bombay, on which
occasion he was knighted. To commemorate his work
as Governor a medical college was built in India and
dedicated to him. He wrote several hymns, twelve
being published by his brother Lord Glenelg in 1839,
the year after he died. However, this hymn, 'O worship
the King,' which was published in Henry Bickersteth's
Christian Psalmody in 1833, the year before Sir Robert
left to take up his post as Governor of Bombay, is the
only one that has remained as a lasting memory to him.
It is based on Kethe's version of Psalm 104 in the *Anglo-
Genevan Psalter* of 1561, which is an appreciation of
God through his creation. God not only creates, but
maintains his creation, and the hymn highlights the fact
that this is God's delight as in these — what I think
are — simply gorgeous lines:

The earth with its store of wonders untold,
Almighty, thy power hath founded of old;
Hath stabilished it fast by a changeless decree,
And round it hath cast, like a mantle, the sea.
Thy bountiful care what tongue can recite?
It breathes in the air, it shines in the light;
It streams from the hills, it descends to the plain,
And sweetly distils in the dew and the rain.

The thought of the unknown psalmist, which is so well
reflected in Sir Robert's hymn (with acknowledgements
to William Kethe), is expressed in a poetic summary of
the creation of the Almighty which is recorded in the

first chapter of the Holy Scriptures.

The tune invariably used with this hymn is 'Hanover'. There's some doubt as to its composer. It first appeared in the sixth edition of Brady and Tate's *A Supplement to the New Version of Psalms* in 1708. The eminent Dr Lightwood gives the credit to William Croft (as do earlier manuscripts), a distinguished musician of the eighteenth century who was organist at Westminster Abbey and composer to the Chapel Royal. In his early days he wrote for the theatre but his major works were for the Church. Handel regarded his music as a 'model for style'. However, John Wesley christened it 'Tally's' possibly under the impression it was by Thomas Tallis. For some time it was thought to be the work of Handel because it was called 'Hanover', but as he did not come to England until 1710 this is unlikely, because the tune in this collection was published two years earlier.

Praise God from whom all blessings flow

Praise God from whom all blessings flow;
Praise him all creatures here below.
Praise him above ye heavenly host;
Praise Father, Son, and Holy Ghost.

The godly and much revered Bishop Ken sang this
doxology at least three times every day of his life as a
priest of the Church of England.

Praise God from whom all blessings flow,
Praise him all creatures here below.
Praise him above ye heavenly host;
Praise Father, Son and Holy Ghost.

It is recorded that it was his custom to use it as the
conclusion of the Morning, Evening and Midnight
hymns. He was a great believer in the singing of hymns
and used to instruct the scholars of Winchester College,
'Be sure to sing the Morning and Evening hymn in your
chamber devoutly.' There have been doxologies from
the days of the Early Church, at first used only by
bishops, then priests, and eventually members of the
congregation. It is not certain when the Bishop wrote
this doxology but there is a record of it being used in
1674 when he published *A Manual of Prayers for the use
of the Scholars of Winchester College*.

Perhaps the time of greatest importance when it was
sung was at Queen Victoria's Diamond Jubilee service
in front of St Paul's Cathedral when, according to *Harper's Magazine* of December 1897,

There were 10,000 people singing 'Praise God, from whom all blessings flow' as loudly as they could, and with tears running down their faces . . . There was probably never before such a moment in which so many races of people, of so many castes, and of such different values to this world, sang praises to God at one time and in one place, and with one heart.

Probably the most frequent use of this doxology was at one of John Wesley's meetings when the congregation sang it every time a person was converted, and in one service it was sung no less than eighty-five times! I wonder what time they went home!

The hymn-writer James Montgomery described it as a 'masterpiece at once of amplification and compression: amplification on the phrase "Praise God" repeated in each line; and compression by exhibiting God as the object of praise, for all his blessings, by every creature here below and in heaven above.'

Thomas Ken who was born in July 1637, at Little Berkhamsted, lost both of his parents early in his life so he went to live with his sister Anne and her husband Isaac Walton. Young Thomas who thus came under the influence of the author of *The Compleat Angler* and his literary friends, as well as having access to Isaac Walton's library, would have to come to know the writings of men like George Herbert and John Donne. After Oxford he took holy orders, eventually becoming chaplain to Bishop Morley which resulted in a long association with Winchester.

One of his additional charges as chaplain was to care for the souls of the parish of St John-in-the-Stoke, and one day he baptized a five-year-old boy who was a paralytic, as well as being deaf and suffering from epileptic fits. To the astonishment of the villagers a few days later when the boy was addressed by his nickname he said in a clear and audible voice: 'My name is not

Tattie. My name is Matthew, Dr Ken baptized me.' And from then on not only could he speak but also walk and he was free from fits!

Rock of ages

1 Rock of ages, cleft for me,
   Let me hide myself in thee;
   Let the water and the blood,
   From thy riven side which flowed,
   Be of sin the double cure,
   Cleanse me from its guilt and power.

2 Not the labour of my hands
   Can fulfil thy law's demands;
   Could my zeal no respite know,
   Could my tears for ever flow,
   All for sin could not atone;
   Thou must save, and thou alone.

3 Nothing in my hand I bring,
   Simply to thy cross I cling;
   Naked, come to thee for dress,
   Helpless, look to thee for grace;
   Foul, I to the fountain fly;
   Wash me, Saviour, or I die.

4 While I draw this fleeting breath,
   When mine eyes shall close in death,
   When I soar through tracts unknown,
   See thee on thy judgement throne;
   Rock of ages, cleft for me,
   Let me hide myself in thee.

This is one of the best-known hymns, and the one with
the most romantic story surrounding it. The author was
also a colourful character with something of a vicious
streak about him. His vitriolic pamphlets attacking the
Wesleys for their Arminian (the doctrine of man's free

choice in respect of his redemption) views certainly makes him an unattractive individual for my book.

The author, Augustus Montague Toplady, was born in Farnham, Surrey, in 1740 in the home of an officer of His Majesty's Army. His father, a major, was killed in the siege of Cartagena a year after Augustus was born. He was a teenager when he went to Ireland with his mother, and studied at Trinity College, Dublin. When in Ireland he happened to attend an evangelistic meeting in a country barn where James Morris, a Methodist lay preacher, was the speaker. This resulted in his conversion, and in 1762 he was ordained in the Church of England. He was appointed curate at Blagdon, Somerset, in 1762 and in 1770 he moved to Devon where he became vicar of Broadhembyry and where he remained for five years. However, he had become a Calvinist (the doctrine that says man is pre-destined to eternal salvation) and ended his ministry at the chapel of the French Calvinists in Orange Street, London, where his life came to an end in dramatic fashion. He had fallen sick to tuberculosis and in his weakened condition unwisely preached a fervent sermon which resulted in his death on 18th July 1778.

There is a legend that he wrote the hymn when he was curate at Blagdon and was sheltering from a storm in the nearby rocky gorge called Burrington Combe in the Mendip Hills. However, the facts are that he wrote the hymn some twelve years after this event. Of course, an experience of sheltering from a storm, which could be vicious in these hills, could have sown the seed that eventually inspired him to write these lines, and it would be a nice thought if that were so. However, he did attach a note to the hymn stating that if sins multiplied with every second in a person's life, by the time a boy was ten years old, he would be chargeable with 315,036,000 sins. It's not known how he arrived at that figure, but his hymn is certainly fully occupied with the subject of sin. Here he emphasizes that we are not able to pay the price of our sins and says that the only hope is that which is expressed in the words of Isaiah (53:6) 'the Lord hath laid on him the iniquity of us all'.

Other references are Moses striking the rock in the wilderness in response to the complaints of the Israelites which resulted in a large gushing of water. This is followed by reference to the blood and water pouring out of Jesus' side when the Roman soldier pierced him with his spear as he hung on the Cross.

It is a most moving hymn in spite of Toplady's hard attitude towards those who did not agree with him theologically.

Souls of men, why will ye scatter?

1 Souls of men, why will ye scatter
   Like a crowd of frightened sheep?
   Foolish hearts, why will ye wander
   From a love so true and deep?

2 Was there ever kindest shepherd
   Half so gentle, half so sweet,
   As the Saviour who would have us
   Come and gather round his feet?

3 There's a wideness in God's mercy,
   Like the wideness of the sea;
   There's a kindness in his justice,
   Which is more than liberty.

4 There is plentiful redemption
   In the blood that has been shed;
   There is joy for all the members
   In the sorrows of the Head.

5 For the love of God is broader
   Than the measures of man's mind;
   And the heart of the Eternal
   Is most wonderfully kind.

6 If our love were but more simple,
   We should take him at his word,
   And our lives would be all sunshine
   In the sweetness of our Lord.

I have always believed that this magnificent hymn, also
known as 'There's a wideness in God's mercy', filled

with the good news of Christ's redemptive work, was
the product of someone with a burning passion for the
souls of men in the evangelical arm of the Church. But
then when I delved into the life story of the author,
Frederick William Faber, I discovered it was one of the
Brompton *Oratory Hymns of 1854*.

Most hymnals now use only eight of the thirteen
verses he originally wrote, and I have no doubt that
they have been used many times during the 'appeal' or
'invitation to the mercy seat' in Salvationist meetings
and evangelistic crusades. The 'evangelical' style of the
hymn is more easily understood when you know something of the upbringing of the author. Faber was born
on 28th June 1814 in Calverley, near Leeds, Yorkshire,
into a Christian home whose parents were strict Calvinists. He was taught from early life that Roman Catholi-
cism was a heresy, and when he was twenty-four he
produced a thesis entitled 'The Ancient Things of the
Church of England' in which he argued in favour of the
Reformation and set out to prove that the Roman
Church was not only unsound but guilty of 'adding
falsehood to the sacraments'.

Then he went to Oxford University where he
encountered the Oxford Movement. He was to sit under
the eloquent preaching of John Henry Newman with
the result that it was to change the whole course of his
life. Before his days at Oxford were over he was to
come to the conclusion that the Anglican Church was
placing too great an emphasis on personal salvation.
This in itself was not its greatest drawback, but that
it was promoted at the expense of the liturgical and
sacramental teachings of such new found heroes as
Keble, Pusey and Newman.

After his graduation he served as curate for the village
of Elton, Huntingdonshire, where he exercised a strong
influence towards the moral reformation of the community. But as time went by he turned more and more

to the practice of Rome which he found increasingly attractive to his changing theology. So it was that in 1845, when he was thirty-one, he scandalized many of his fellow-Anglicans by being re-baptized in the Roman Catholic Church. Subsequently with his baptized name of Wilfrid he founded a community known as 'Brothers of the Will of God' who later became known as the 'Wifridians'. Father Wilfrid, as he was then known, was both an eloquent preacher and author of many much loved hymns, including the favourite of many Protestant churches, 'My God how wonderful thou art'. He was honoured with the degree of Doctor of Divinity by the Pope, and appointed Superior of the Roman Catholic Brompton Oratory in London. However, he was not to live for many more years. He died at the Oratory when he was only forty-nine. It must have been a throw-back to his early evangelical upbringing that his great ambition as a Catholic priest was to encourage his people in their devotion to God by the use of his hymns, no doubt remembering how much the strong teaching he had experienced through the hymns had influenced him in his youth.

I was also impressed by the fact that he gave this hymn the simple title: 'Come to Jesus'. The tenderness and consuming love that he must have felt for his wayward parishioners is seen in these opening lines, 'Souls of men why will ye scatter, like a crowd of frightened sheep?' This is, of course, Faber's reflection of Jesus as the great Shepherd, but he also draws many of his thoughts from the Book of Job where this devout man explores the limitlessness of God with such lines as 'The measure thereof is longer than the earth, and broader than the sea' (Job 11:9).

Take my life and let it be

1 Take my life, and let it be
Consecrated, Lord, to thee;
Take my moments and my days,
Let them flow in ceaseless praise.

2 Take my hands, and let them move
At the impulse of thy love;
Take my feet, and let them be
Swift and beautiful for thee.

3 Take my voice, and let me sing
Always, only, for my King;
Take my lips, and let them be
Filled with messages from thee.

4 Take my silver and my gold,
Not a mite would I withhold;
Take my intellect, and use
Every power as thou shalt choose.

5 Take my will, and make it thine;
It shall be no longer mine:
Take my heart, it is thine own;
It shall be thy royal throne.

6 Take my love; my Lord, I pour
At thy feet its treasure store:
Take myself, and I will be
Ever, only, all, for thee.

Frances Ridley Havergal and her father, Canon William Havergal, were responsible for very many popular hymns, and this one may have been the most successful.

It was written as result of a very bold prayer which Frances made in the privacy of her room at a house party in Areley House in London when she joined ten other guests for a five-day holiday. She was of the opinion that none of the other guests had the relationship with Christ which she would have liked them to have so she prayed for them.

This is her own account of what happened:

I went for a little visit of five days. There were ten persons in the house; some were unconverted and long prayed for, some converted but not rejoicing Christians. He gave me the prayer, 'Lord, give me all in this house'. And he just did. Before I left the house, everyone had got a blessing. The last night of my visit I was too happy to sleep and passed most of the night in renewal of my consecration, and these little couplets formed themselves and chimed in my heart one after another till they finished with — 'ever, only, all for thee!'

This happened in the early days of February 1874.

Frances Havergal was born at Astley in Worcestershire on 4th December 1836. Her spiritual appetite showed itself at the early age of four when she not only took to reading but memorizing portions of Scripture. This was soon followed by an ability to write verse, both of which skills were encouraged by her father. She was not blessed with good health but in spite of that she became expert in Greek and Hebrew and some modern languages. But she was plagued by doubts in her youth about her spirituality. There was an emphasis in some church circles at the time that only a special group of Christians would be counted in the 'elect' of God, and Frances feared she would not qualify. However, this was soon resolved as indicated by this quote from a letter to a friend: 'There and then I committed my soul to the Saviour, and earth and heaven seemed bright from that moment.' This reminds me of a story that the great Baptist preacher, Charles Hadden Spurgeon — at the height of his success preaching to thousands in his Tabernacle at Elephant and Castle, London — would be attacked by doubts as to whether or not he was a Christian. In his vestry before entering his pulpit he would kneel in prayer with his Bible open at the verse: 'Believe on the Lord Jesus Christ, and thou shalt be saved.' He said, 'I would pray the penitent's prayer concluding with "I believe".' He would then rise to his feet and announce to the devil, 'Now that makes it sure I am a Christian.' Whenever the doubts returned, he would apply the same remedy. Frances was also a gifted musician and soloist and sought after as a concert soloist which she put aside because she did not believe that is what God wanted her to. In August 1878 she wrote to a friend:

The Lord has shown me another little step, and, of course, I have taken it with extreme delight. 'Take my silver and my gold' now means shipping off all my ornaments to the Church Missionary House, including a jewel cabinet that is really fit for a countess, where all will be accepted and disposed of for me . . . Nearly fifty articles are being packed up. I don't think I ever packed a box with such pleasure.

It is not well known that Frances wrote her own commentary on her hymn in which she highlights the different aspects of consecration in the life of a Christian:

Consecration is not so much a step as a course; not so much an act, as a position to which a course of action inseparably belongs . . .
We do not want to go on taking a first step over

and over again. What we want now is, to be maintained in that position, and to fulfil that course.

I was intrigued to read once of Miss Havergal's practice to distribute cards on which one of her hymns was printed with a space for a signature below it. Then after explaining the meaning and significance of the hymn she would invite those present to sign in the space provided. Perhaps that is how she discovered that all present at the house party had decided to commit their lives to Christ.

Two of the many hymns she wrote that I have always found make a helpful contribution to an act of worship when they have been sung are:

1. 'Like a river glorious'. She wrote this at Leamington on 3rd November 1874 when suffering from the dreadful sickness of typhoid. In a letter the following year to Esther Beamish she shared the fears that had overwhelmed her at the time. These continued until she found the peace available, as the hymn says, 'hidden in the hollow of his blessed hand'.

2. 'Lord speak to me that I may speak' was written at Winterdyne in April 1872 headed 'A Worker's Prayer. None of us liveth unto himself' (Romans 14:7).

She spent the latter days of her life in a house on the brow of a hill above Caswell Bay in the Gower peninsula overlooking the Bristol Channel where she died on 3rd June 1879.

Tell out my soul

1 Tell out, my soul, the greatness of the Lord!
Unnumbered blessings give my spirit voice;
Tender to me the promise of his word;
In God my Saviour shall my heart rejoice.

2 Tell out, my soul, the greatness of his name!
Make known his might, the deeds his arm has
   done;
His mercy sure, from age to age the same;
His Holy name — the Lord the Mighty One.

3 Tell out, my soul, the greatness of his might!
Powers and dominions lay their glory by;
Proud hearts and stubborn wills are put to flight,
The hungry fed, the humble lifted high.

4 Tell out, my soul, the glories of his word!
Firm is his promise, and his mercy sure:
Tell out, my soul, the greatness of the Lord
To children's children and for evermore!

The late Sir John Betjeman in a broadcast in 1976
described this hymn as 'one of the very few new hymns
really to have established themselves in recent years'.
Yet its author, Timothy Dudley-Smith, had not
intended it to be a hymn, in fact, he was not a hymn-
writer at the time. He said, 'I did not think of myself
as having the gifts of a hymn-writer when in May 1961
I was reading a review copy of the New English Bible
New Testament in which that line ('Tell out my soul,
the greatness of the Lord') appears. I saw in it the first
line of a poem, and speedily wrote the rest.'

It is a metrical paraphrase of the Magnificat which I

like to think is the last Old Testament psalm and the first New Testament hymn, an inspired bridge. . . .

The Virgin Mary having been told that she was to bear a child who would be the Son of God hurried into the hill country of Judah to her cousin Elisabeth to share the exciting news. In response to Elisabeth's greeting Mary exclaimed: 'Tell out, my soul, the greatness of the Lord, rejoice, rejoice, my spirit, in God my saviour; so tenderly has he looked upon his servant, humble as she is' (Luke 1: 46–48) NEB.

At the time, Timothy Dudley-Smith, who is now Bishop of Thetford, was on the staff of the Church Pastoral Aid Society and living in Vanbrugh Park, Blackheath (the first home of his married life).

Later, someone brought it to the notice of the compilers of the *Anglican Hymn Book* who asked if they could include it as one of the hymns in their next edition. This encouraged Bishop Dudley-Smith to write more hymns, in fact more than 130 in the following twenty years.

He was born in Derbyshire and encouraged in his love of poetry by his schoolmaster father. He was ordained in 1950 and in addition to parish work he served as head of the Cambridge University Mission in Bermondsey from 1953 to 1955.

Our paths crossed when I was Administrative Secretary at the Evangelical Alliance and Timothy was chairman of our Literature Committee. He had previously served on the EA staff as Editorial Secretary which included the post of editor of the monthly magazine *Crusade*, published following Dr Billy Graham's first London Crusade. From the EA he went to CPAS and then to Norwich as Archdeacon followed by his consecration as Bishop of Thetford in 1981.

Most of his hymns have been written in the picturesque village of Ruan Minor, Cornwall, where with his wife and three children he has spent summer holidays since 1969. His hymns have been included in upwards of eighty hymnals worldwide, and I was surprised to discover that all this has been achieved even though (I have it on good authority) he claims to be tone deaf!

Two tunes are generally used for the hymn.

'Tell out my soul' was composed for these words by Michael Baughen, Bishop of Chester, and a friend of the author.

'Woodlands' is the other tune which was married to the hymn by the editors of *100 Hymns for Today*. This was composed by Walter Greatorex, at one time Director of Music at Gresham's School in Norfolk, where 'Woodlands' is the name of one of the houses.

The day of resurrection

1 The day of resurrection!
  Earth, tell it out abroad;
  The passover of gladness,
  The passover of God!
  From death to life eternal,
  From earth unto the sky,
  Our Christ hath brought us over
  With hymns of victory.

2 Our hearts be pure from evil,
  That we may see aright
  The Lord in rays eternal
  Of resurrection light;
  And, listening to his accents,
  May hear, so calm and plain,
  His own 'All hail!' and, hearing,
  May raise the victor strain.

3 Now let the heavens be joyful;
  Let earth her song begin;
  Let the round world keep triumph,
  And all that is therein;
  Let all things seen and unseen
  Their notes of gladness blend,
  For Christ the Lord hath risen,
  Our Joy that hath no end.

St John of Damascus is the writer of this hymn; it was
extracted from his Golden Canon by John Mason Neale
who translated it from Greek and expertly formed it
into verse. In its original form there were nine odes
based on the nine biblical canticles used in the Greek
rite on Easter Day. Neale based this hymn on the first

ode of the canon which takes the account of the
Israelites emerging victoriously from the bed of the Red
Sea as a symbol of Christ's resurrection. St John was
known as the 'last of the Greek Fathers'. The ruthless
Emperor Constantine hated him and sought to kill him,
so he took refuge in the monastery of Mar Sabas situ-
ated between Jerusalem and the Dead Sea. By all
accounts it was a dreadful place — a lonely forbidding
building on a high ridge overlooking the Kedron Valley
said to stand 'clinging to the face of a steep precipice,
so that it is difficult to distinguish man's masonry from
the natural rock', with jackals scowling in the gorge
below ready to pounce on any scraps of food thrown
out by the monks. It is all the more significant that such
a magnificent work of sacred poetry, considered to be
the finest in the Greek Church, should have come out
of so dismal and foreboding a place as this stark building. It is especially telling that its subject should be the
story of the resurrection. The triumph of beauty and
goodness over the ugliness of evil.

As the Golden Canon of St John of Damascus is sung
in Greece this is how one onlooker described the scene
recorded in John Mason Neale's publication *Hymns of
the Eastern Church*, of 1862:

The scene is at Athens. As midnight approached, the
Archbishop, with his priests, accompanied by the
King and Queen, left the Church . . . Everyone now
remained in breathless expectation, holding their
unlighted tapers in readiness . . . Suddenly a single
report of a cannon announced that the twelve o'clock
had struck, and that Easter Day had begun. Then the
old Archbishop elevating the Cross, exclaimed in a
loud exulting tone, 'Christos anesti' — Christ Is
Risen! — and instantly every single individual of all
that host took up the cry, and the vast multitude . . .
with one spontaneous shout of indescribable joy and

triumph, 'Christ is risen! Christ is risen!' At the same moment the oppressive darkness was shattered by a blaze of light from thousands of tapers . . . sending streams of fire in all directions . . . bands struck up their gayest strains; the sound of the trumpets and the roll of the drums echoed through the town as the cannon announced to those far and near glad tidings of great joy — 'Christos anesti!' Christ is risen.

In this hymn of great rejoicing we are reminded of the words of Psalm 118 (verse 24): 'This is the day that the Lord has made. We will be glad and rejoice in it.' Coupled with the words of St John: 'From death to life eternal, from earth unto the sky, our Christ hath brought us over with hymns of victory', we can link the words of Jesus in John 3: 16: 'For God loved the world so much that he gave his only Son so that anyone who believes in him shall not perish but have eternal life' (TLB).

The old rugged cross

1 On a hill far away stood an old rugged cross,
The emblem of suffering and shame;
And I love that old cross where the dearest and best
For a world of lost sinners was slain.
So I'll cherish the old rugged cross
Till my trophies at last I lay down;
I will cling to the old rugged cross
And exchange it some day for a crown.

2 O, the old rugged cross, so despised by the world,
Has a wondrous attraction for me;
For the dear Lamb of God left his glory above
To bear it to dark Calvary.
So I'll cherish . . .

3 In the old rugged cross, stained with blood so
divine,
A wonderous beauty I see;
For 'twas on that old cross Jesus suffered and died
To pardon and sanctify me.
So I'll cherish . . .

4 To the old rugged cross I will ever be true,
Its shame and reproach gladly bear;
Then he'll call me some day to my home far away,
When his glory for ever I'll share.
So I'll cherish . . .

I have strong childhood memories of this popular
gospel song being sung by John McCormack on a brittle
78 rpm record playing through a horn speaker attached
to a wind-up gramophone. It was usually accompanied
by my mother's untrained, yet pleasantly sounding

voice as she busied herself around the house. In spite of the spate of new gospel and worship songs that flow through our churches and homes these days it is surprising that this song still finds its way to the top of the polls of favourites conducted by my colleagues in the BBC. As Ken Osbeck, an American hymnologist, says: 'Seldom can a song leader suggest a time for favourites from any congregation without receiving at least one request for "The Old Rugged Cross". It is generally conceded to be one of the most popular of all twentieth-century gospel songs.'

It was composed by the American George Bennard, who was born in Youngstown, Ohio, in 1873. Following his personal commitment to Christ as a young man he joined the Salvation Army and was trained as an officer. Both he and his first wife were officers in the Salvation Army, serving in North America for several years before he sought to be ordained in the Methodist Episcopal Church. He took part in itinerant evangelistic work in Michigan and New York during this time. It was during one of his missions that he passed through an intense period of suffering, which caused him to compare his experience with Christ's crucifixion when he was studying Paul's reference to the fellowship of Christ's suffering in his letter to the Philippians, 'That I may know him, and the power of his resurrection, and the fellowship of his sufferings, being made conformable unto his death; if by any means I might attain unto the resurrection of the dead' (3: 10–11). This caused him to undergo a significant change in his thinking because he had previously been inclined to look upon the Cross as a symbol, but now through his personal experience he saw it as being the very heart of the Gospel.

This is how he described how he came to write the words of 'The Old Rugged Cross':

The inspiration came to me one day in 1913, when I

was staying in Albion, Michigan. I began to write
'The Old Rugged Cross'. I composed the melody
first. The words I first wrote were imperfect. The
words of the finished hymn were put into my heart
in answer to my own need. Shortly thereafter it was
introduced at special meetings in Pokagon, Michigan,
on 7th June 1913. The first occasion where it was
heard outside of the church at Pokagon was at the
Chicago Evangelistic Institute. There it was introduced before a large convention, and soon it became
extremely popular throughout the country.

During the remaining forty years of evangelistic work
he composed other gospel songs. He lived until he was
eighty-five and died on 9th October 1958 in his home a
few miles north of Reed City, Michigan. A twelve-foot
cross engraved with the words 'The Old Rugged Cross'
has been erected outside his house on the roadside.
The scripture on which he based 'The Old Rugged
Cross' was from 1 Peter 2:24: 'He personally carried the
load of our sins in his own body when he died on the
Cross' (TLB).

His friends said that the last verse with the refrain
aptly sums up the life of the Revd George Bennard who
wrote: 'To the old rugged cross I will ever be true.'

What a friend we have in Jesus

1 What a friend we have in Jesus,
  All our sins and griefs to bear!
  What a privilege to carry
  Everything to God in prayer!
  O what peace we often forfeit,
  O what needless pain we bear —
  All because we do not carry
  Everything to God in prayer!

2 Have we trials and temptations?
  Is there trouble anywhere?
  We should never be discouraged:
  Take it to the Lord in prayer!
  Can we find a friend so faithful,
  Who will all our sorrows share?
  Jesus knows our every weakness —
  Take it to the Lord in prayer!

3 Are we weak and heavy-laden,
  Cumbered with a load of care?
  Precious Saviour still our refuge,
  Take it to the Lord in prayer!
  Do thy friends despise, forsake thee?
  Take it to the Lord in prayer!
  In his arms he'll take and shield thee,
  Thou wilt find a solace there.

Joseph Scriven was the author of this simple but most reassuring hymn of comfort to the countless number of people who have sung it. And to know something about this man is to understand its success in becoming the favourite of such devoted Christians as my dear mother. She, like many other wives and mothers in the

Second World War, had reason to derive comfort from its lines when she found herself an early widow and with a son away on war service in the Far East.

Joseph was born in 1819 into a wealthy home in Banbridge, County Down, in the northern part of Ireland. But the life he was to lead in Canada, by his own choice I would add, was in direct contrast. When he was once seen in a street in Bewdley North, Port Hope, in Ontario, he was carrying a saw and carpenter's horse. A visiting businessman inquired: 'Who is that man? I want him to work for me.' But he was told: 'You can't get him. He saws wood only for poor widows and sick people who cannot pay.'

After his studies in Trinity College, Dublin, he entered the Addiscombe Military College near where I live in Surrey. However, his health prevented him completing a military career and he returned to Trinity as one of the College lecturers. It was whilst he was there that he fell deeply in love with a beautiful Irish girl and she returned his love. They could hardly wait to get married. But the evening before their wedding day he was devastated by the news that she had tragically lost her life; she had been drowned in an accident. So it was that Joseph emigrated to Canada, and after a period as tutor to children of a retired naval officer, decided to give his energies in the service of the poor, according to the teachings in the Sermon on the Mount, and joined the Plymouth Brethren. But even there he was to experience another loss. He met another young lady whom he decided to marry, only to lose her after a brief illness.

Through his service to the poor in Port Hope he became known as 'the man who saws wood for poor widows and sick people who are unable to pay', and he was often seen giving his clothing to those who had none and were suffering from the icy cold Canadian winters. In fact, this puzzled many people who did not

know him, thinking he was an eccentric bachelor and
unaware of the sad events in his past.

One day news came to him from Ireland that his
mother was very ill. He was distressed at being unable
to return to her in Ireland, so he decided the best he
could do would be to write to her with some words of
comfort. With the letter he enclosed the words of this
hymn which he had written for her personally and not
intended for publication.

Some time later he fell ill himself and when a friend
visited him he noticed a rough piece of paper on the
table alongside his bed. On it were written the words
of this hymn. His friend picked it up, read the verses,
and asked Joseph if he were the writer. 'Well, not completely,' Joseph quietly replied, 'The Lord and me did
it between us.'

Years later Ira Sankey, D. L. Moody's associate,
found the words printed anonymously and included it
in his *Gospel Hymns and Sacred Songs* in 1875, attributing
it to Horatius Bonar whom he had met in Edinburgh
two years earlier. Dr Bonar quickly told Sankey that he
was not the author, so for the following two years the
author was shown as anonymous until the publishers
McGranahan and Stebbens discovered it had been written by the modest Joseph Medlicott Scriven.

His life ended shrouded in mystery. In October 1886
he rose from a sick bed and for some unknown reason
left his house. The following day he was found
drowned in the waters of the nearby Rice Lake. The
people of Bewdley erected a monument to their 'Good
Samaritan' friend.

When all your mercies, O my God, my rising soul surveys

1 When all your mercies, O my God,
  My rising soul surveys,
  Transported with the view, I'm lost
  In wonder, love, and praise.

2 Unnumbered comforts on my soul
  Your tender care bestowed,
  Before my infant heart conceived
  From whom those comforts flowed.

3 Ten thousand thousand precious gifts
  My daily thanks employ,
  Nor is the least a cheerful heart
  That tastes those gifts with joy.

4 Through every period of my life
  Your goodness I'll pursue,
  And after death, in distant worlds,
  The glorious theme renew.

5 Through all eternity to You
  A joyful song I'll raise;
  For O eternity's too short
  To utter all Your praise!

At half-past four in the morning one day last summer, my wife Joan and I were on the top of Mount Neissen in Switzerland awaiting the sunrise. As the rays of the sun spread before us a breathtaking view of a range of mountains, pointed up by the peaks of the Mönch, Eiger and Jungfrau changing from one glorious colour into another, I could understand the thoughts of Joseph

Addison as he took the thoughts of David as a basis for his paraphrase in this hymn. David wrote: 'The heavens claim God's splendour, the sky speaks of his handiwork; day after day takes up the tale, night after night makes him known; their speech has never a word not a sound for the ear, and yet their message spreads the wide world over, their meaning carries to earth's end . . . (Psalm 19 — Moffatt), and it continues in this wonderful vein (worth reading at any time).

Joseph, along with his friend Sir Richard Steel, started the magazine *The Spectator* in 1711, and a year later on 9th August he published this hymn in its columns under the title, 'Gratitude'. He added these words:

> If gratitude is due from man to man, how much more from man to his Maker! Every blessing we enjoy, by what means soever it may be derived upon us, is the gift of him who is the great Author of good and Father of mercies.

He has been described as the bright star of early eighteenth-century literature, and said that his purpose in publishing his essays in his periodical was: 'The great and only end of these speculations is to banish vice and ignorance out of the territories of Great Britain.'

It is a remarkable thing, even a tribute to both men, that though their publications were the required reading of Britain's fashionable women and the habitués of London's coffee houses, they did not avoid challenging the extreme political corruption of the time. Even so it was said that 'the most cruel pamphleteers respected him' for his unsullied life and abilities. It is certain that the hymns of Isaac Watts exercised a great influence over him, who also greatly admired him as 'the most authentic judge of fine thought and language that our age has produced'. John Wesley also held both him and his friend Steele in high esteem saying they were the first sign of calling society to take account of spiritual values and the good life of respectable morals.

He did not live a long time — he was only forty-nine when he died in 1719 — but as he believed God is good, just and a rewarder of those faithful to him, so he endeavoured to live a good life by example. 'When he was about to die,' says his biographer Hippolyte Taine, 'he sent for his step-son, Lord Warwick, whose careless life had caused him some uneasiness. He was so weak that at first he could not speak. The young man, after waiting a while, said to him: "Dear sir, you sent for me, I believe; I hope that you have some commands; I shall hold them most sacred." The dying man with an effort pressed his hand and replied gently: "See in what peace a Christian can die." '

Joseph Addison was born in Milston, a village near Amesbury, Wiltshire, on 1st May 1672. His father, the Very Revd Lancelot Addison, was at one time the dean of Lichfield. Joseph went to Charterhouse and Queen's and Magdalen Colleges, Oxford, with the intention of taking holy orders. However, he found himself inclined to politics and literature. He subsequently became a Fellow of Magdalen, a Commissioner of Appeals, Under Secretary of State, and finally, in 1708, a Member of Parliament. He died in Holland House, Kensington, on 17th June 1719 and was honoured by burial in Westminster Abbey.

When I survey the wondrous cross

1 When I survey the wondrous cross
  On which the Prince of glory died,
  My richest gain I count but loss,
  And pour contempt on all my pride.

2 Forbid it, Lord, that I should boast,
  Save in the death of Christ my God:
  All the vain things that charm me most,
  I sacrifice them to his blood.

3 See from his head, his hands, his feet,
  Sorrow and love flow mingled down:
  Did e'er such love and sorrow meet,
  Or thorns compose so rich a crown?

4 Were the whole realm of nature mine,
  That were an offering far too small,
  Love so amazing, so divine,
  Demands my soul, my life, my all.

Charles Wesley wrote 9000 poems, of which 6500 were used as hymns, but he once said that he would gladly exchange them all in exchange for the privilege of writing this hymn.

Isaac Watts was, of course, the author. He was born on 17th July 1674 into a seafaring family, his grandfather being Commander of a warship under Admiral Blake. However his father, known as Enoch Watts, was disinclined to go to sea and became a humble clothier, and a deacon at the city's independent chapel at Above Bar. He was a strong-minded father and prepared to go to prison on two separate occasions because of his religious convictions. He dissented with the Act of Uniformity. Isaac was a precocious child with a penchant for versifying to such an extent that Enoch threatened to whip him if he continued to answer his father in rhyme, whereupon the young lad cried out in tears:

> O father, do some pity take,
> And I will no more verses make.

Thereupon, I imagine the father gave him up as a hopeless case. It certainly caused him to respond to his son's complaint after church one Sunday that 'old Barton's psalm doth send us to sleep', that they should take up pen and write something better. And young Isaac, sixteen at the time, did just that later in life — when he was thirty-one he gave us this magnificent and deeply moving hymn. However, I prefer his original words for the second line of the first verse: 'Where the young Prince of Glory died'. Sadly, two years later in 1709, he bowed to the criticism of his friends and changed the words to their present form.

He composed this hymn for use in a communion service having been inspired by Paul's immortal words to the Galatians (6:14): 'God forbid that I should glory, save in the Cross of our Lord Jesus Christ.'

It is not without significance that Watts, who had a comprehensive knowledge of English, should use the word 'survey'. This goes beyond a glance at the Cross. It says that we linger long and meditate upon the sight of Jesus on the Cross. And I like his earlier thought of the 'young man' from heaven giving his life as an atonement for the sins of his Father's creation.

Another strong phrase in the first verse is 'pour contempt on all my pride'. It presents such a vivid picture of the penitent before the Cross treating with utter disdain any thought that he possessed any righteousness worthy to be offered in place of the complete sacrifice before him. Paul had been proud of his Jewish line of descent, a Pharisee of the Pharisees, but here he turns it on its head as he stands before the Cross. Here he knows that he dare not boast of any attainment. I find the culmination in the final verse of such a complete and utter surrender in response to such love most compelling.

Isaac Watts was not merely a theorist. He was willing to work out his Christian faith in a life of dedication. He was also a dedicated student and early in life was fluent in Greek, Latin and Hebrew. In fact he so impressed the family doctor and some friends that they were ready to give him the opportunity of studying at Oxford with a view to ordination in the Church of England. He declined because of his allegiance to his father's nonconformist convictions. In the end he was given an education at the nonconformist college of Thomas Rowe. In 1696 he joined Dr Chauncey at Mark Lane Independent Chapel, London, and in 1702 succeeded him as its pastor. Sadly he failed to enjoy good health, but through the kindness of his friends Sir Thomas and Lady Abney was able to spend the latter part of his life in their country home free of the pressures of pastoral duties. He died at Stoke Newington on 25th November 1748 and is buried in the well-known Puritan cemetery Bunhill Fields, in City Road, London, a must for American tourists!

When peace like a river

1 When peace like a river attendeth my way,
  When sorrows like sea-billows roll;
  Whatever my lot you have taught me to say,
  'It is well, it is well with my soul.'

2 Though Satan should buffet, if trials should come,
  Let this blessed assurance control,
  That Christ has regarded my helpless estate,
  And has shed his own blood for my soul.

3 My sin — O the bliss of this glorious thought —
  My sin — not in part — but the whole
  Is nailed to his cross; and I bear it no more;
  Praise the Lord, praise the Lord, O my soul.

4 For me, be it Christ, be it Christ hence to live!
  If Jordan above me shall roll.
  No pang shall be mine, for in death as in life
  You will whisper your peace to my soul.

5 But Lord, it's for you — for your coming we wait,
  The sky, not the grave, is our goal:
  O trump of the angel! O voice of the Lord!
  Blessed hope! blessed rest of my soul.

In common with many other hymn-writers Horatio
Spafford, the author of this hymn popular with the
'freer' of the Free Churches, suffered a series of tragedies ending with the drowning of his four daughters *en
route* from the USA to the United Kingdom.

Horatio, who was born on 20th October 1828 in North
Troy, New York, took up residence in Chicago when a
young man and began a successful practice as a lawyer.

He belonged to the Presbyterian Church but was also an active supporter of the world-renowned Baptist evangelist Dwight L. Moody, whose headquarters and Bible institute were in Chicago. In addition to his active lay ministry in his church and his support for the Moody evangelistic campaigns he was a very successful and prosperous businessman and invested heavily in properties in Chicago especially in the valuable areas alongside Lake Michigan.

His first grief came with the death of his only son. Then, shortly afterwards, in 1871, Chicago was swept by a vicious fire which destroyed a large part of the city and completely wiped out all the properties which he owned.

Two years later Moody and Sankey set out for the British Isles to conduct their evangelistic meetings, and Spafford agreed to travel with them as an assistant. He arranged for his wife and four daughters to accompany him in November of that year and made the necessary sailing arrangements. However, just at the last minute there were serious developments in his business in Chicago which meant that he had to remain behind planning to follow them in a few days. Mrs Spafford and her daughters excitedly boarded the SS *Ville du Havre* unaware of the tragedy that was to befall them on the twenty-second day of the month when a British ship, the *Lochearn*, collided with their ship and within twelve minutes it sank completely. The survivors were taken to Cardiff but only Horatio's wife could be found among them. Later it was discovered that all their daughters had gone down with the ship, and Mrs Spafford had the unenviable task of breaking the news to her husband. She cabled him the sad news in two words, 'Saved alone'. Mr Spafford hurriedly set sail for Britain to join his wife and it is said that as his ship passed over the spot where his daughters had been drowned his thoughts were of his sorrows like 'the sea billows', and he was moved to write:

> When peace, like a river, attendeth my way,
> When sorrows like sea-billows roll;
> Whatever my lot, you have taught me to say,
> It is well, it is well with my soul.

Although the background to the hymn is one of sadness, the words of the writer and sufferer are not morbid and self-pitying, but full of hope. In his third verse Horatio directs our thoughts to the suffering of Christ as God's work of redemption for mankind. In a much smaller sense all suffering can have a redemptive quality in it if we are prepared to follow the way of the Cross.

Sadly, Mr Spafford's trouble did not end there. Maybe the tragedies of his life more seriously disturbed the sensitivity of this creative man's mind than was realized by his wife and friends, and towards the end of his life he had delusions of grandeur imagining that he had been chosen to be the second Messiah and he went to live in Jerusalem where he died in 1888 at the age of sixty.

When we walk with the Lord (Trust and obey)

1 When we walk with the Lord
In the light of his word,
What a glory he sheds on our way!
While we do his good will,
He abides with us still,
And with all who will trust and obey.
  Trust and obey,
  For there's no other way
  To be happy in Jesus,
  But to trust and obey.

2 Not a shadow can rise,
Not a cloud in the skies,
But his smile quickly drives it away;
Not a doubt nor a fear,
Not a sigh nor a tear,
Can abide while we trust and obey.
  Trust and obey . . .

3 Not a burden we bear,
Not a sorry we share,
But our toil he doth richly repay;
Not a grief nor a loss,
Not a frown nor a cross,
But is blest if we trust and obey.
  Trust and obey . . .

4 But we never can prove
The delights of his love,
Until all on the altar we lay;
For the favour he shows,
And the joy he bestows

Are for them who will trust and obey.
  Trust and obey . . .

5 Then in fellowship sweet,
  We will sit at his feet,
  Or we'll walk by his side in the way.
  What he says we will do,
  Where he sends we will go,
  Never fear, only trust and obey.
    Trust and obey . . .

Testimony-time in churches seems now to have largely
disappeared. I was familiar with this type of church
meeting in my youth, and we used to call it RFA time —
'Reading For Anything'. This was a feature of the
Wesley class meetings, and Christians were called upon
to witness to their faith in open-air gatherings without
any notice. Part of my training at the Elim Bible College
in the days immediately after the Second World War
was to accompany that great saint Joseph Smith, Dean
of the College, to Speaker's Corner at Hyde Park,
London, for a weekly open-air meeting. I noticed that
the professional hecklers were always quiet when a
testimony was given. They found it hard to argue with
personal experience. St Paul was the supreme example
of giving his testimony. When he did so before King
Agrippa, the king said: 'Almost you persuade *me* to be
a Christian.'

This hymn, which was a great favourite with Moody
and Sankey, is truly a 'Testimony Hymn'. In fact the
inspiration for it came to Mr Moody's song leader,
Daniel Towner, during their evangelistic campaign in
Brockton, Massachusetts in 1866.

This is Daniel's account of how it came to be written:

Mr Moody was conducting a series of meetings in

Brockton, Massachusetts, and I had the pleasure of singing for him there. One night a young man rose in a testimony meeting and said: 'I am not quite sure — but I am going to trust, and I am going to obey.' I just jotted that sentence down, and sent it with the little story to the Revd J. H. Sammis, a Presbyterian minister. He wrote the hymn, and the tune was born.

In fact, Daniel Towner was the one who composed the tune.

John Sammis, the author, came from Brooklyn, New York, where he was born in July 1846. In his twenties he became a successful businessmen as well as an active Christian layman. But his Christian activities so filled his life that he felt called to leave his business and serve as a secretary with the YMCA. When in his thirties he felt another call of God, this time to enter the Presbyterian Church, and after a necessary period of college training in the year 1881 he was ordained a Presbyterian minister. After a number of pastorates he joined the staff of a theological college in Los Angeles as a teacher and it was whilst he was there that he received the request of Daniel Towner to write a hymn based on the words of the young man in the Massachusetts meeting.

The composer of the tune to this song, Daniel Towner, was responsible for the tunes of more than 2000 gospel songs. In addition to his work with D. L. Moody he exercised a strong influence on evangelical church music in the States. Later he was appointed as the first head of the Music Department at the Moody Bible Institute in Chicago where he trained ministers of music, and this soon developed into being an essential part of American church life. One of his students was Charles Alexander.

After John Sammis received his friend's request the first lines that came to his mind formed themselves into

the refrain: 'Trust and obey — for there's no other way.
To be happy in Jesus, but to trust and obey.' Then the
words of the Old Testament prophet Samuel came to
his mind as he continued to think on the simple statement of the young man in Massachusetts:

> And Samuel said, 'Hath the Lord as great delight in
> burnt offerings and sacrifices, as in obeying the voice
> of the Lord? Behold, to obey is better than sacrifice,
> and to hearken than the fat of rams' (1 Samuel 15:22).

Gradually he developed the conditions on which that
trust and happiness flourishes. It involves doing the
will of God, then trust and obedience will drive the
shadows and clouds away. Obedience is better than
sacrifice said the prophet, so it is ourselves that we
should first place on the altar of God. Finally, to be at
God's bidding and go where he says we should go, is
the secret of the Christian's success. When the Israelites
followed God's way in their journey through the wilderness they were safe. It was only when they went their
own way that they ran into trouble.

Who would true valour see (He who would valiant be)

1 Who would true valour see,
  Let him come hither;
  One here will constant be,
    Come wind, come weather;
  There's no discouragement
  Shall make him once relent
  His first avowed intent
    To be a pilgrim.

2 Whoso beset him round
  With dismal stories,
  Do but themselves confound;
    His strength the more is.
  No lion can him fright,
  He'll with a giant fight,
  But he will have a right
    To be a pilgrim.

3 Hobgoblin nor foul fiend
  Can daunt his spirit;
  He knows he at the end
    Shall life inherit.
  Then fancies fly away;
  He'll fear not what men say;
  He'll labour night and day
    To be a pilgrim.

John Bunyan wrote these words around the story of Mr Valiant-for-Truth in his Pilgrim's Progress. During Bunyan's day the singing of hymns in church was not accepted by all Christians and although he favoured singing in church he firmly maintained that this should be confined to metrical psalms. It took a self-confessed agnostic, Ralph Vaughan Williams, who lived near the friendly village of Capel where I also once lived, to set this to music. He was greatly interested in folk-songs and one day in 1904 he was in a hamlet called Monk's Gate, near Horsham in Sussex, and heard a ploughman sing an old folk-song, 'Our Captain calls all hands aboard'. At the time he was helping Canon Percy Dearmer with *The English Hymnal* and arranged Bunyan's words to this tune which he subsequently named 'Monk's Gate'.

Dearmer felt that it would be audacious for a congregation to sing such a boastful song as 'one here will constant be, come wind, come weather'. So he changed the words to 'let him in constancy follow the Master'. However, he had misinterpreted Bunyan's message which was meant to say: 'Please pay special attention to Mr Valiant-for-Truth, if you want to see the kind of courage that is essential to the Christian character.' Happily, editors of other hymn-books have used Bunyan's version. Anyhow, I thought it worth mentioning that which explains why the hymn has two different versions: Bunyan's 'who would true valour see', and Dearmer's 'He who would valiant be'.

The hymn occurs at an exciting time in the Pilgrim's story. Valiant had, in common with other fighters for truth, encountered three gangsters at Deadman's Corner who have the fantastic names of Wildhead, Inconsiderate, and Pragmatic. They try to divert him from his courage — and if you want to know more, read *Pilgrim's Progress*.

This hymn warns us not to throw in our lot with the Wildhead, the fanatics, or those insensitive to the needs of the poor, or those who follow the dictates of expediency rather than policy. It calls for Pilgrim to exercise control. No coward can be a Christian — 'no lion can him fright'. Valiant's death scene made such an impression on Bernard Shaw that he asked that it should be read aloud at his funeral.

John Bunyan led a colourful life. He was born in Elstow in Bedfordshire on 30th November 1628 and was trained as a tinsmith by his father. But when he was sixteen he was conscripted for the parliamentary army under Sir Samuel Luke. Some say he went with the army to Ireland where it was disbanded when he was nineteen and then he returned home to Bedford to marry a remarkable woman 'without so much as a dish or a spoon between them'. But his wife did bring with her two books, *The Plain Man's Pathway to Heaven*, by Arthur Dent, and *The Practice of Piety*, by Lewis Bayly. This was to have a greater impact on his life than anything else she could have possessed. Sadly she died when he was only twenty-eight leaving him with four children. However she lived long enough to see her husband undergo a spiritual conversion, and become an itinerant preacher.

A year after she died he was ordained as a Baptist minister; but, preachers of dissenting churches were prohibited from preaching, a factor which Bunyan ignored, and this resulted in his imprisonment on several occasions. During these imprisonments he wrote some of his books, including the first part of *The Pilgrim's Progress* (part 1 in 1678 and part 2 after his release in 1684). One hundred thousand copies were sold in the first ten years, and millions since. It seems he was given a great deal of freedom in prison because he is said to have married again in 1661 when a prisoner. When on a mission of mercy in London in 1688 he caught a chill through riding in wet weather and died on 31st August. He is buried in Bunhill Fields.

Index of Writers

Acknowledgements

'O Soul, Are you weary and troubled' by Helen Lemmell © 1922, 1950 Singspiration Music Inc. All rights for UK and Eire administered by United Music Publishing Ltd. Reprinted by permission of Boosey & Hawkes Music Publishers Ltd. 'Tell out, my soul' © Timothy Dudley-Smith, Rectory Meadow, Bramerton, Norwich, NR14 7DW. 'O Lord my God' by Stuart K Hine © 1953 Stuart K Hine/Thankyou Music, PO Box 75, Eastbourne, East Sussex, BN23 6NW, used by permission. 'From Heaven You Came' by Graham Kendrick © 1983 Thankyou Music. Used by permission. 'Morning Has Broken' by Eleanor Farjeon © David Higham Associates. 'Christ is the World's Light' by Fred Pratt-Green © Stainer & Bell Ltd. The publishers have made every effort to trace copyright holders. In the case of any omissions, please contact them and acknowledgement will be included in any reprint of this book.